How to Get a Job If You're a Teenager

Cindy Pervola and Debby Hobgood

Alleyside Press®

Fort Atkinson, Wisconsin

Contents

For Jessi, my wonderful teenage daughter
Cindy Pervola

For Sue and Kristin, my cheerleaders
Debby Hobgood

Published by Alleyside Press, an imprint of Highsmith Press
Highsmith Press, W5527 Highway 106, P.O. Box 800
Fort Atkinson, Wisconsin 53538-0800   1-800-558-2110

© Cindy Pervola and Debby Hobgood, 1998

The paper used in this publication meets the minimum requirements of American National Standard for Information Science — Permanence of Paper for Printed Library Material. ANSI/NISO Z39.48-1992.

Library of Congress Cataloging-in-Publication Data

Pervola, Cindy
    How to get a job if you're a teenager / Cindy Pervola and Debby Hobgood.
        p.   cm.
    Includes bibliographical references and index.
    Summary: A basic job skills guide for teenagers with appendices of additional resources
and web sites for job searches.
    ISBN 1-57950-013-7 (soft : alk. paper)
    1. Applications for positions. 2. Job hunting. 3. Vocational guidance. 4. Employment interviewing.
    5. Business etiquette. 6. Teenagers--Employment. [1. Applications for positions. 2. Job hunting
    3. Vocational guidance. 4. Employment interviewing.]
    I. Hobgood, Debby. II. Title.
    HF5383.P44 1998
    650.14'0835--dc21   97-45843
                                           CIP

Introduction

Anyone can open up a newspaper and find a job in the want ads or at the mall, but not everyone will be able to get those jobs, especially if they don't know how. The whole process of getting a job can be a little intimidating, especially if you've never completed a job application.

This book will take you through the whole process, and show you how to get, and *keep* a job. It will also help you find a job that will suit your interests and personality.

One teenager, Erin, applied for a job in her frayed jeans, a tight tank top, her tongue pierced, her nose pierced twice and a string of earrings along one ear. That might be okay if she was applying for a job at a body piercing shop, but Erin wanted a job at her favorite retail clothing store at a nearby mall. She dressed like that to shop there and the employees were always friendly with her. Erin thought she should "be herself."

The problem was that she didn't give the employer a good first impression. Erin wasn't a customer any more. She was applying for a job. She wanted to be an employee there. She needed to sell herself to the employer and try to show what a good employee she would be if she got the job. Erin needed to realize that she couldn't dress for a job the way she dressed to go to school or shopping. Even though employers want you to "be yourself," they also want you to be professional.

Besides her appearance, Erin wasn't prepared to be interviewed on the spot. She went to pick up an application right after school and didn't realize that she needed to take some things with her. As a result, she didn't have any of the information needed to complete the application. She hadn't thought about things like how she would get to work every day or which hours she would be available to work. The employer was left with the impression that Erin didn't really care whether she got that job or not.

Erin didn't have the "tools." She didn't know what to do or how to do it. This book will give you the tools for being successful, not only in your job search, but in the work force and with your future career. These are tools that you need when you go hunting for a job today, and the same tools you will need when you're 35 and need to find a job. There are many unemployed college graduates out there and some of them just don't know the simple rules covered in this book.

How to Get a Job if You're a Teenager is a basic guide to what every teenager should know before entering the job market. There are seven chapters which are to-the-point, easy-to-read, and focus on what *teenagers* want and need to know to be better prepared for all aspects of entering the work force.

The first chapters focus on finding out which jobs are interesting and right for you. A brief personality questionnaire helps to match your interests with specific jobs and suggests areas you might be interested in pursuing. We show you how to find out which businesses are hiring and explore the possibility of going into business for yourself. We cover the basic rules and courtesies when picking up applications and include sample resumes.

The third chapter takes you through each step in completing an application, from filling in your name and address to the open-ended question at the end, with a sample application at the end of the chapter. We highlight details that are important to employers, such as printing neatly, using a blue or black pen and checking your spelling.

Chapter 4 explains how to go about preparing yourself for the interview and provides tips that will impress employers. It explains how to prepare to ask questions during the interview to get the answers that *you* want to know, for instance, "Is there a dress code?" or "What is your policy on jewelry?" At the end of this chapter, a section on researching the company on the Internet and at the library is included. The more you know about the company interviewing you, the more comfortable you will feel. You will also be better equipped to ask questions of your own during the interview.

Chapter 5 is about the interview itself. It covers what you should wear, basic courtesies such as shaking hands, eye contact, and most importantly, a list of typical questions you might be asked. Knowing what to expect and being able to think about the answers to questions beforehand will make you feel more at ease during the interview. We also offer suggestions on how to answer those questions. We suggest questions of your own to ask, (including how and when to bring up the uncomfortable subject of money), and what to do when the interview is over. Going in for an interview can be a nerve-racking experience, so we give you tips on what you can expect and how to relax and present yourself well.

Chapter 6 is titled Congratulations, You Got the Job!, and it describes what to expect on your first day. We tell you what you will need to take on your first day, describe the forms you will need to complete, tell you about training manuals, time cards, and explain what a probationary period is.

Just about anybody can get a job, but keeping a good job that you enjoy is preferable to getting any old job that happens to be available. It reflects on the next job you'll get, and the next one and the next one. Employers look for "job stability" (whether or not you can keep a job), so we show you what will help you keep your job and what makes someone a "good employee."

The last chapter discusses leaving a job on a positive note, how to give a two week notice, and alternatives to quitting. Appendices include additional resources on employment (including websites) and sources of state and federal employment information.

Using the information in this book will give you the tools to succeed in your job search or at your job now, and throughout your life, whenever you need to find a job. If you know what to do, what is expected of you and the "rules" of a job search, you increase your ability to land and keep the job you want. *Good luck.*

You Want to Get a Job. So Now What?

You're ready to work. You've got your eye on a car, or maybe you just want some extra cash for concerts, movies, new clothes and CDs. Maybe you want a summer job, or a part-time job after school and on weekends. Whatever the situation, what you want is your *own* money, and a job is the way to earn it.

But what if this is the first time you've looked for a job? What if you've never filled out an application before? How do you find out who's hiring? What should you wear to the interview? What kind of questions will they ask and how should you answer them?

So, where do you start? First of all, you need to decide what kind of job is right for you. Think about what you like to do or what type of jobs look like fun or seem interesting. Look at the places where your friends work and ask them if they like their jobs. If you like busy places with lots of people, then consider restaurant or retail work. Or, if you want to be working outdoors, you'll want to look into jobs at amusement parks, water parks, plant nurseries, or jobs doing yard work. Look into jobs that you think you'd enjoy. If you're a vegetarian, for example, why would you apply for a job cooking hamburgers?

Think about what kind of career work interests you. For instance, if you think you might like to teach, apply at a day care center, a preschool, or as a tutor. If you think you'd like to be a veterinarian, apply at veterinary clinics, pet stores or at a zoo. Pick up the telephone and call photographers in your area if you're interested in photography. They might need someone to run errands or do odd jobs. If you enjoy your work, chances are you'll work harder and do a better job. Focus on *your* interests.

The following personality quiz will help you learn more about yourself. Check the boxes that best describe *you*. This will help you concentrate on which jobs might suit you the best. If you are willing to consider many jobs, or if you're not sure you're interested in a particular job, check it anyway. That will give you more job options to consider.

Personality Quiz

❏ **A.** I enjoy physical activity.

❏ **B.** I like to be around a lot of people.

❏ **C.** I have a lot of energy.

❏ **D.** I like to be around children.

❏ **E.** I enjoy being outside.

❏ **F.** I like to talk on the telephone.

❏ **G.** I would like a desk job.

❏ **H.** I am a quiet person.

❏ **I.** I like to fix things and figure out how things work.

❏ **J.** I like being around and taking care of animals.

This personality quiz will help you focus on jobs which suit you best.

Evaluate your answers

If you checked A, B or C:

You probably are an outgoing, energetic person. Consider applying at retail stores, grocery stores, bakeries, fast food and restaurant businesses, including ice cream and coffee shops. You could be a cashier, salesperson, stock person, bagger, food server, cook, caterer, baker, host/hostess or bus person. Perhaps working at a health club, country club, bowling alley, movie theater or a hotel would also interest you. These are businesses with lots of activity.

If you checked D:

Add camp counselor, day care centers, babysitting, tutoring and giving lessons (swimming, ice skating, roller blading, foreign language) to that list since you also like being around children.

If you checked E:

If your main interest is working outdoors, consider applying at amusement parks, miniature golf courses, sports stadiums, a zoo, a petting zoo, a water park, as a lifeguard, at plant nurseries, at parks doing landscaping, construction work, or yard and farm work. Other outdoor work that might appeal to you would be house painting or newspaper delivery. These jobs tend to be more physical but there are opportunities to work around a lot of people or just a few, depending on your preference.

> *My first job was at an amusement park because I wanted to be outside all summer. The first year wasn't very much fun because I had to do all the boring jobs but the second summer was better. I got to pick which games I wanted to work since it was my second year.*
>
> Jessi, age 16.

If you checked F, G or H:

If you'd prefer a desk job and would rather be indoors in an office setting, consider applying as a receptionist, for clerical or computer work (with temporary agencies, banks or large corporations), in telemarketing, with a typing service or work at a library. There's a lot of activity going on at these jobs but it's indoor work. Keep in mind that you'll probably have to dress a little more formally in these types of jobs.

If you checked H:

If you prefer to work alone, you can work in an office setting or outdoors. Consider computer or clerical work, newspaper delivery, housecleaning, auto detailing, or start your own business by offering a service.

If you checked I:

If you're more mechanically minded, consider applying for jobs at body shops, factories, as a mechanic or gas station attendant, any kind of repair service or as a delivery person. Jobs doing yard or farm work might appeal to you, too.

If you checked J:

If you think you'd like working with animals, apply at zoos, petting zoos, at veterinary clinics, or at area farms. You could even start your own pet sitting business.

These suggestions are only meant as a guide to help narrow down the options to jobs you think would most interest you. If you have a job in mind that isn't on the list, by all means go for it.

Hopefully, you now have an idea where you would like to apply for a job.

I applied at a graphic design firm because I like to draw. Mostly, I ran errands but I got to see what they did. Once they used me in some photographs they needed for an annual report. I got paid extra and it was fun.

John, age 17.

Jobs generally not open to teenagers

- Any mine or quarry
- Hazardous factory work
- Plants manufacturing explosives
- Plants manufacturing iron or steel
- Sawmills or logging
- Any job involving exposure to lead, or to dangerous or poisonous dyes or chemicals
- Oil refineries
- Any job requiring the use of dangerous machinery
- Any job that involves exposure to radioactive material
- Roofing work
- Any job requiring the use or carrying of firearms or other weapons

How do I find out who's hiring?

One of the best ways to find a job is by **word of mouth**. Ask your friends and your family if they know of any places looking for help.

Your high school or college is a good place, too. Check out signs posted on **bulletin boards** and ask the **guidance counselor or employment counselor** at your school. Many area businesses call high school and colleges and tell them of any openings they have, so job postings at your school are an excellent way to find a job.

Many schools also have **programs that allow students to work in an industry or job** related to occupations in which they are interested in pursuing, *and* get credit for it at the same time. These programs help students decide if the career they are considering is right for them by giving them hands-on experience. Usually, there is a teacher or counselor specifically in charge of this program. (In some areas, this is called cooperative education, or "co-ops.") For instance, if you're interested in studying photography, you might get a job with a photographer. You may get paid and get school credit for working there. The school won't necessarily find a job for you, but counselors and teachers can make suggestions and point you in the right direction.

 **Good Idea**

Apply to several businesses where you're interested in working. Some places may not be hiring at the time you apply or some may only have one or two positions open.

Many businesses advertise by putting a **sign in their window**, but if there isn't a sign, that doesn't mean that they are not hiring. Always apply to any place of business where you think you'd like to work, whether there's a sign in the window or not.

Some businesses advertise in the **want ads in the local newspaper**.

Shopping malls occasionally have **"Job Fairs"** where you can fill out applications with a variety of businesses that are hiring. These job fairs are usually advertised in the newspapers and at the malls. Sometimes they do on-the-spot interviewing so be prepared for that. Check out the **information desk at shopping malls,** too. They usually know which stores are looking for help.

Some **employment agencies** might be helpful. These businesses help people find jobs but there could be a charge for their service, so make sure you ask. Look under "employment agencies" in the yellow pages and get in touch with the ones that handle part-time or temporary help. Most of the other agencies are for professionals or for people with certain skills. You could check under "Employment Services - Government" in the yellow pages, too.

If there is a large company nearby where you'd like to apply, call and ask for their **personnel department.** You will want to first ask if they have any job openings for teenagers. If so, you will need to ask where you should go to fill out an application.

Many jobs are also posted on the **Internet**, and the websites listed at the end of this chapter can provide good leads.

Be an entrepreneur and work for yourself

You can also get a job outside of a commercial business by **starting your own business**. There are lots of opportunities babysitting, doing yard and farm work, and doing odd jobs for friends or elderly neighbors. If you would rather go that route, you can find many good suggestions in the resources listed at the end of this chapter (Creating Your Own Job). As a businessperson, you can sell your services in several ways. First, let people know that you babysit, mow lawns, run errands, do odd jobs, etc., by sending out flyers in your neighborhood. Your flyer should have your name, your telephone number, and the services that you provide. Second, you could write a list of references on a separate sheet of paper to hand out. These would be people who have hired you, and have been happy with your work. But, always ask their permission first. You can note in your flyer that references are available.

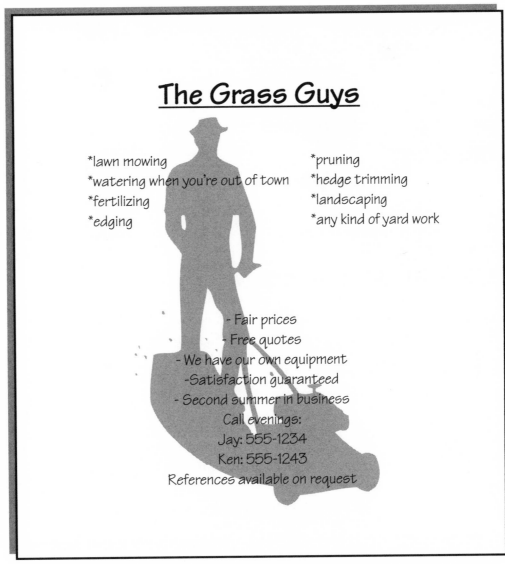

The Grass Guys

*lawn mowing
*watering when you're out of town
*fertilizing
*edging

*pruning
*hedge trimming
*landscaping
*any kind of yard work

- Fair prices
- Free quotes
- We have our own equipment
-Satisfaction guaranteed
- Second summer in business
Call evenings:
Jay: 555-1234
Ken: 555-1243
References available on request

Promotional Flyer: Send flyers out in your neighborhood to let people know which services you provide. You could also look into posting them on bulletin boards in local grocery or hardware stores.

Use your imagination with your own business: house sitting, pet sitting, grocery shopping or running errands (maybe for elderly or business people). Think about other services you could offer: house cleaning, garage cleaning, fence or house painting, car washing and detailing, pool service, or party helper. Think about what you like doing or the work you have done for others that drew compliments, and start your own business.

💡 Good Idea

> Take a class in your area of interest (babysitting, carpentry, landscaping). People are more likely to hire you if you have had training.

"I got my first job through the co-op program at school. It was great because I got out of school early and went straight to work. I worked in a men's formal wear store for two years until I graduated. They offered me a position as an assistant manager but I turned it down because I wanted to go to college. It was great experience, and it looks good on my resume."

Nathan, age 19.

How much can I expect to be paid?

Most businesses start teenagers out at minimum wage, especially if it's their first job. If you have experience or live in a big city, you can expect to make a little more. If you're in business for yourself, try to determine a fair hourly rate or a per job rate for what you do. Ask friends and neighbors how much they pay to have their lawn cut or what they pay a babysitter. That will give you a starting point on setting your fee.

"I started my own yardwork business when I was 15. Now, I own a landscaping business."

Jeff, age 39.

You should now have a good idea where you'd like to work, how to find out who's hiring and how much you'll probably get paid. The next step is picking up the applications.

Resources on Job Opportunities

Compiled by Donna McMillen

Look for the following resources (or others similar to them) at your school library or counseling center and in public libraries. Check the World Wide Web for the websites and their links.

Summer or Part-time Jobs and Other Opportunities

Guide to Accredited Camps 1997/98. 41st ed. Martinsville, IN: American Camping Association, 1989. This annual guide has over 2,000 accredited camps, retreat, reunion and seminar locations listed by state with information on address, phone number, when established, activities, emphasis, employment opportunities and contact person. Indexed by activities, special needs, day camps. Write to camps directly for further employment information. *Note:* Call the American Camping Association for a free copy of ACA's *Summer Camp Employment Booklet* at 317-342-8456 ext. 331.

Peterson's Summer Opportunities for Kids and Teenagers 1997. 14th ed. Princeton, NJ: Peterson's, 1997. Directory information on academic programs, travel adventures, and camps including arts, special interest, sports, wilderness, special needs, religious, and programs abroad. Includes details on activities, dates, costs, financial aid, job opportunities, accreditation, and contact information.

Summer Jobs for Students 1997. 46th ed. Princeton, NJ: Peterson's, 1997. Annual guide lists opportunities with camps, ranches, resorts, conference centers, tours, national parks, summer theater, amusement parks, and covers a wide variety of jobs from arts and crafts instructors to wranglers. Contains general and employment information, benefits, contact address, and a note from the employer.

Woodworth, David, ed. *Overseas Summer Jobs 1997.* 28th ed. Princeton, NJ: Peterson's, 1997. Thousands of summer opportunities abroad are listed by country along with a description of the employer, positions offered, requirements, minimum age, and contact information. Includes a section on au pair, paying guests, and exchange visits.

Websites

Cool Works: <http://www.coolworks.com>. Seasonal jobs in national parks

The Teenager's Guide to the Real World Online!: Information About Summer Jobs: <http://www.bygpub.com/books/tg2rw/summer-jobs.htm>. Excellent website with summer job hunting advice and numerous links to summer job websites for camps, park services, internships, and more.

Find other websites by searching with the terms "summer" and "jobs."

Local Opportunities

Local newspapers—Check the yellow pages of the telephone book under Newspapers to find out what your local papers are, or ask at the library. Some cities will have local employment papers in addition to the daily paper. Major papers now often have websites with updated help wanted classified ads. Some neighborhoods have a monthly paper or newsletter in which you can place a job wanted ad or find ads for help wanted.

Parks and Recreation Directories—Check under city, county, and state listings in the government pages of your local phone book to find listings for parks and recreation departments. See Summer Jobs for Students (above) for national parks.

Restaurant and Theater Chains—Check in the yellow pages in your local phone book under Restaurants and Theaters-Movies to find local places for possible jobs.

Temporary Services for Teens—Check in the yellow pages of the phone book under Employment Agencies and Employment Contractors-Temporary Help for local agencies or look in the help wanted section of your local newspaper.

Regional Guides

The Insider's Guide series, published by Surrey Books, has job-hunting guides for Atlanta, Greater Boston, Chicago, Dallas/Fort Worth, Europe, Houston, New York area, Pacific Rim, San Francisco area, Seattle/Portland, Southern California, and Washington, DC. These guides contain detailed information on all aspects of the job hunt including career selection, regional business trends, top companies, websites, resumes, interviews, summer/temporary/part-time jobs, how to handle a new job, professional organizations, and listings for thousands of the region's employers giving address, phone and jobline numbers when available.

JobBank series, published by Adams Media Corporation, contains job hunter's information for major employers, industry associations and publications, and temporary agencies. Each volume targets a city or metropolitan area such as Greater Philadelphia, Northern New England, Las Vegas, Seattle and others. Basics of job hunting are followed by overviews of the major employers by type of business.

State Job Service Listings

State Leadership Directory: Directory III: Administrative Officials 1997. Lexington, KY: The Council of State Governments, 1997. Contains official names, addresses, phone numbers, and fax numbers for each state for these departments which may be useful to the job hunter: child labor, employment services, equal employment opportunity, job training, labor, occupational safety, and parks and recreation.

Check the government pages of your phone book for local addresses of city, county, and state employment services. Check for state and local websites which may have job listings.

Creating Your Own Job

Bernstein, Daryl. *Better Than a Lemonade Stand: Small Business Ideas for Kids.* Hillsboro, Or: Beyond Words Pub., 1992. Includes small business suggestions including dog walker, birthday party planner, and photographer.

Drew, Bonnie and Noel Drew. *Fast Cash for Kids: 101 Money-Making Projects for Young Entrepreneurs.* Hawthorne, NJ: Career Press, 1991. Includes basic information for starting a business and 101 ideas including pool cleaning, selling mistletoe, storm clean-up and bike repairs.

Jones, Vada Lee. *Kids Can Make Money Too!: How Young People Can Succeed Financially.* Menlo Park, CA: Calico Paws Publishing: 1987. Money management, over 200 ways to make money, and helpful hints for running your own business.

Mariotti, Steve. *The Young Entrepreneur's Guide to Starting and Running a Business.* New York: Random House, 1996. Advice on starting your own business is highlighted by stories of entrepreneurs such as Berry Gordy and Bill Gates, and case studies of particular businesses including t-shirt maker, babysitting, plant care, house cleaning, sound and lighting, grooming service, pet care, handmade crafts or food, messenger service, and more. Lists of further resources, how to raise capital, and how to write a business plan are included.

Menzies, Linda, Oren S. Jenkins, and Rickell Rae Fisher. *A Teen's Guide to Business: the Secrets to a Successful Enterprise.* Large print ed. Thorndike, ME: Thorndike Press, 1992. Includes choosing a job, part-time jobs that lead to careers, the job hunt, working life, managing stress and time, how to start and run your own business, and legal matters.

Riehm, Sarah L. *50 Great Businesses for Teens.* Old Tappan, NJ: Macmillan, 1997. Creative guide for setting up your own business includes ideas for outdoor or indoor work, school-based ventures, special skills, computer skills, errand or delivery services, mail order, and holiday ventures. Includes bookkeeping and accounting, publicity, government and tax requirements, and how to get started. (A previous book by the same author was: *The Teenage Entrepreneur's Guide: 50 Money-making Business Ideas.* Chicago: Surrey Books, 1990.)

Thompson, Terri. *Biz Kids' Guide to Success: Money-Making Ideas for Young Entrepreneurs.* Hauppauge, NY: Barron's, 1992. Ideas and how-to's for young people wanting to start their own business including money basics, marketing, and complying with legal requirements.

Internet Guides

Glossbrenner, Alfred and Emily Glossbrenner. *Finding a Job on the Internet.* New York: McGraw-Hill, 1995. This how-to guide covers Internet basics from buying a modem to exploring America Online (AOL) Career Center, Online Career Center (OOC), the *Occupational Outlook Handbook* online, finding jobs in various fields, online resumes, contacts, and online databases.

Gonyea, James C. *The On-Line Job Search Companion: A Complete Guide to Hundreds of Career Planning and Job Hunting Resources Available Via Your Computer.* New York: McGraw-Hill, 1995. Book includes software disk for America Online for Windows, information on career planning and job hunting, and an extensive list of resources in multiple media formats including bulletin board services, on-line network services, audiocassettes, and software.

Riley, Margaret, Frances Roehm and Steve Oserman. *The Guide to Internet Job Searching.* Lincolnwood, IL: NTC Publishing Group, 1996. How to search for jobs on the Internet, including federal, state, and local websites, bulletin boards, and other job listing sites.

Websites

Use the Internet guides above to find website addresses for local companies which may have an employment link on their home page.

America's Job Bank: <http://www.ajb.dni.us/html/seekers.html>. Includes job listings, *Occupational Outlook Handbook*, occupational projections by state, and employers' websites.

Career Magazine: <http://www.careermag.com>. Articles and information on job openings, employers, resume bank, job fairs, and site of the week.

CareerMosaic: <http://www.careermosaic.com/cm/>. Links to job openings by career field and geographic area.

CareerPath: <http://www.careerpath.com/info.html>. Job postings through newspaper websites across the nation.

Entry Level Job Seeker Assistant: <http://members.aol.com/Dylander/jobhome.html>. Job links and basic assistance for job seekers who have never had a job in their field or who have less than a year of non-academic experience.

Getting Real: <http://www.gettingreal.com/tools/emtool.html>. **My Tools by Emily** includes links for starting on a career path, resumes, interviews, job hunting, internships, and alternatives to college.

IntelliMatch: <http://www.intellimatch.com/>. Job listings, employer profiles, resumes.

JobSmart Home: <http://jobsmart.org/>. Links to sites for resumes, career guides, salary information, the hidden job market, and job openings in California.

The Monster Board: <http://www.monster.com/>. More than 50,000 job listings including entry level jobs, internships, and links to other job search websites.

The Riley Guide: Employment Opportunities and Job Resources on the Internet: <http://www.dbm.com/jobguide/>. Links to websites for job listings, resumes, specific occupational areas, research on careers, and career selection.

Virtual Job Fair: <http://www.vjf.com/>. Includes top websites for job listings, business research, associations, state and federal career resources, and employment services.

Picking Up the Application

2

Be ready to be interviewed when you go to pick up an application. An employer might have the time to talk to you when you complete it, especially if you have given a good first impression. First impressions are formed immediately, so what you wear to pick up the application is just as important as what you wear to an interview.

What should I wear?

The best advice is to dress conservatively. There's no need to wear a suit and tie or a dress, but it's not a good idea to pick up an application in cutoffs and a T-shirt either. A safe bet is to wear something in between. Pants and a button down shirt work well, (girls could wear a skirt instead of pants), or even a pair of jeans is okay as long as they aren't old and worn and the place of business is casual. Dressing nicely to pick up the application shows that you care about making a good first impression. It shows that you want the job. Think about the times you have judged someone, good or bad, because of what that person was wearing. Employers will do the same thing with you. They will look at what you are wearing and how you present yourself, and make a decision, usually within several minutes, as to whether or not they are interested in hiring you. This is especially true in a business where you would be dealing directly with their customers.

> *I didn't go out and buy all new clothes. I wore a nice sweater, a new pair of jeans and some nice shoes to pick up my applications.*
>
> Nicole, age 15.

Suggestions for Girls

Navy, black or khaki twill pants or skirt

Blue jeans (new) or denim skirt

Blouse, shirt or polo shirt

Closed-toe shoes

Matching jacket & stockings or tights if the place of business is formal.

Suggestions for Boys

Navy, black or khaki twill pants

Button down shirt

Polo shirt

Blue jeans (new)

Loafers or closed-toe shoes

Tie and blazer if place of business is formal

When do I ask for an application?

Wait until the person at the place of business isn't helping any customers before you ask for an application, and never ask if you can borrow a pen. Leave the business, (or sit in your car or on a bench outside) to fill the application out, even when you plan on returning it right away. Some businesses might request that you fill the application out on the premises and not take it home. So, make sure you have all the information you will need to fill out an application.

If the employer tells you they aren't hiring at that time, ask when they will be hiring so you will know when to return. Many businesses hire seasonal help. For instance, some businesses start hiring for Christmas help in October. Retail stores also need back to school help and hire for that in June and July. Nurseries and landscaping businesses need most of their help in the spring. Don't give up if they tell you they aren't hiring. Their busy season could be coming.

Good Idea

> If you have a friend or a parent accompanying you, ask them to wait for you outside the place of business. Employers like to see that you can do things on your own.

> **seasonal:** work during a certain time of year, often under 90 days, usually during summer or winter holidays.

Fashion faux pas for picking up an application

Use the same dress code for both picking up an application and for going to an interview.

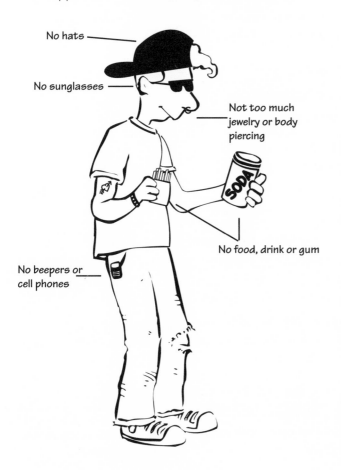

No hats

No sunglasses

Not too much jewelry or body piercing

No food, drink or gum

No beepers or cell phones

Job Applicants Survival Kit

✔ Your own pen (black or blue ink).

✔ Social Security Number (SSN).

✔ List of all the high schools (and colleges) you have attended, with their addresses and telephone numbers, your graduation date and major.

✔ List of previous employers, if any, including their addresses, telephone numbers and supervisors' names.

✔ List of three references , including their addresses and telephone numbers. (You must ask their permission first.)

✔ Dictionary or Spell Check (to check your spelling).

✔ Your availability (when you are available to work each day).

✔ Your start date (when you can start work).

✔ Your alien card if you are not a U.S. citizen.

✔ A good attitude.

Should I call first?

It depends. Many businesses, like fast food businesses, don't like to get telephone calls during certain times of the day. A busy manager has to stop what they're doing to take your call, and sometimes this can be annoying, especially if they have already received twelve calls that morning from people wanting to know the same thing. The best advice is to go in yourself whenever possible. If you live far away or you're pressed for time, it's okay to call first, but try to do so when you think it's most convenient for them. For instance, you wouldn't want to call a fast food restaurant at noon because they will be busy serving lunch.

> *When I was 16, I walked by a store that had a sign in the window that said they needed help. I went in and applied. Today I'm the regional manager.*
> Sue, age 32.

If you do decide to call, find a quiet place by yourself where there is no background noise. Always ask for a manager. (Most of the other employees will not know the answer to your questions.)

It's a good idea, on the other hand, to call the personnel department if you're applying at a big company. They will be able to tell you if they have any openings for teenagers and where you should go to apply. Have a pen and paper ready in case you need directions.

Top 5
Questions to ask when calling about a job

- Are you taking applications at this time?
- Do you have any openings for teenagers?
- Do you need full time or part time help?
- For which shifts are you hiring?
- When is a good time to pick up an application?

What is a letter of recommendation?

A letter of recommendation is a brief letter from an adult (not your parents), that explains why you would be a good employee. It usually states how long the adult has known you and what kind of person you are. If you have a teacher, coach or friend of the family who knows you well, ask if they would mind writing a letter of recommendation for you. It's a good idea to have one, just in case.

Do I need a resume?

Probably not, but you might come across a business that does not have an application for you to complete. In that instance, you would need a resume and maybe a letter of recommendation, too. You might also run into an employer who requests a resume.

resume: a brief summary of your work, education and personal experience and background.

Creating a resume

Contact information: It's a good idea to put your name, address and telephone number in bold print.

Headings: Also put your headings like EDUCATION and WORK EXPERIENCE in bold print or underlined, to highlight them.

Education: Under this heading, list any classes outside of school you have taken such as computer classes, typing class, or vocational or technical training. Any additional classes you have taken make you much more desirable.

Work experience: List jobs you have held beginning with the most recent. Include any volunteer work or community service you have done, even if it was for a short period of time. List jobs you have had outside of commercial businesses such as babysitting or lawn service.

Awards: If you have won awards, title a section AWARDS and list those.

Personal or interests section: Brag about yourself. List sports, clubs and other activities in which you participate, languages you speak fluently, special training you have received, etc. Leave nothing out, no matter how insignificant you think it might be. It says a lot about who you are.

Two sample resumes follow on the next page to give you a better idea what a resume should include.

> *I felt embarrassed giving a resume to the record store owner because I didn't have any work experience. My Mom helped me put one together and it turned out pretty well. I said how much I liked music, and that I was in a band and worked hard. I couldn't believe it when they called me for an interview.*
>
> Eric, age 15.

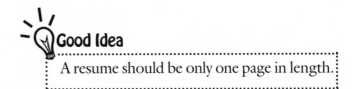

Good Idea

A resume should be only one page in length.

Courtney Parker
400 Washington Street
Springfield, CA 10011
(333) 333-3333

EXPERIENCE

8/97 - present — Springfield High School. Cashier at school store before and after school. Duties include opening and closing registers, handling money and weekly inventory.

6/97 - 8/97 — Pam Donalds. Babysitter for her 5-year-old three mornings a week. Responsible for his overall care and some cooking.

9/96 - 12/96 — Morris Veterinary Clinic. Assistant. Duties included cleaning kennels, feeding and exercising the animals.

5/96 - 9/96 — YMCA summer camp. Volunteer as a counselor in training. Responsible for assisting camp counselors with their duties.

EDUCATION — Currently a junior at Springfield High School.

INTERESTS — Music. Took guitar lessons for two years.
Drawing. Placed first in two district wide shows.
Snowboarding.

Jacob Williams
101 South Street
Springfield, CA 10001
(333) 333-3333

EDUCATION — Freshman at Kane County College. Communications major.

WORK HISTORY

1/96 - present — **Franks Department Store.** Lead cashier in high volume men's clothing department. Responsible for maintaining station, giving direction to cashiers, merchandising, and product knowledge.

2/94 - 1/96 — **Wills Food Store** Stock person, third shift. Duties also included monthly inventories.

8/92 - 5/96 — **Kane County Public Library**. Volunteer work in Ready to Read program teaching reading skills to children as well as adults.

PERSONAL

- ◆ Dependable, hardworking and energetic.
- ◆ Four years of high school Spanish.
- ◆ Active outdoors, with a special interest in biking.
- ◆ Extensive knowledge of WordPerfect, Windows, and Photoshop.
- ◆ Avid reader of mysteries.

Creating a Resume: A resume should be a brief, clear and easy-to-read summary of your work experience, education and personal information.

Filling Out the Application

The two most important things to keep in mind when filling out an application are to be **honest** and to fill it out **completely**. An application is a legal document, and you could get fired for lying on your application.

Employers do not like to see any blank spaces on applications they receive. Every bit of information you can give them about yourself is extremely helpful, so do not leave any questions unanswered.

Complete the application in pen with black or blue ink and get a dictionary or use a spell checker to avoid misspelling. Print neatly and take your time. A sloppy application with words crossed out or misspelled turns off an employer right away, and your application will end up at the bottom of the stack. (You might even ask for two applications if you're prone to making mistakes.)

The following is a guide to filling out a typical application. Every application is a little different but all the basic information is the same. A completed application can be found at the end of this chapter.

Date: Write today's date.

Name: Your full name as it appears on your birth certificate or driver's license. If you go by a nickname, you can put your nickname in parenthesis. For example, you can write, Jacob (Jake) Williams, if you wish to be called Jake.

Social Security Number: If you do not have a social security number, you can find out how to apply for one by calling 1-800-772-1213. You can also look in the phone book for Social Security under "United States Government" for an office close to you. Do not apply for a job until you have a Social Security Number.

> **SSN:** abbreviation for Social Security Number.

Address: Employers want your current address. For example, if you are in college, use your college address. Use your permanent address (or home address) for your tax information.

Telephone number: Write in your home telephone number. Be sure to include a second number if you have two residences. For instance, if your parents are divorced and you spend time with both of them, write in both telephone numbers.

> **applicant:** person applying for a job.

Under 18? The employer wants to know if you will need a work permit. If you are over 18, you don't need a work permit. If you're under 18, you might need one, but it varies with each state. A work permit tells the employer how many hours a day and a week you are allowed to work. Your high school will issue your work permit or they can tell you how to get one.

Are you a U.S. citizen? If you are not a U. S. citizen, the employer will need to see your alien card when you are hired.

Position applied for (or desired): They want to know if you are applying for a sales position, stock person, waiter/waitress, bus person, dishwasher, etc. If you are interested in anything that they have open, it's okay to put "any position available."

Full time, part time, seasonal: They want to know how many hours a week you would prefer to work. Full-time is usually 30–40 hours a week and part time is usually 0–30 hours per week. This will vary with each company. Seasonal refers to temporary work for under 90 days during a certain time of year, usually summer and winter holiday.

Salary desired (or rate of pay requested): Put "minimum wage" if this is your first job. If you have worked before, put the rate of pay when you left your last job. If you feel you were underpaid at your last job or you need extra pay because you will need to use public transportation or have other expenses, add 5%–10% more per hour.

For example, if you were making $6 an hour at your last job as a hostess in a restaurant, you may feel you are worth more than that. Maybe you now have a year of experience and you were very good at the job. You might want to request $6.25–$6.50 an hour on your application. You can also write "negotiable" with good job experience and good references, but make sure you have a specific amount in mind when you go in to be interviewed. Also, be sure you're ready to tell them why you feel you deserve that amount.

"I asked for $1 over minimum wage because I had to take the bus. I live about 45 minutes away but I needed full-time work for the summer and I said I could work any day of the week as long as the buses were running. They needed somebody with experience that could work any time, so they gave me more than minimum wage, but not as much as I requested."

Maria, age 18.

Date available to start work: If you can start working tomorrow, write that date. If you're applying for a seasonal job, put in the date when you can start working. For example, if you are applying for a summer job but don't get out of school for three weeks, write in the date after the last day of school when you can actually begin working. Be specific.

Availability: Here, the employer wants to know specifically when you can work each day of the week. It doesn't necessarily mean that you will be scheduled to work at those times every day. It lets the employer know when or if you could work on those days, if needed.

It is very frustrating for employers when new-hires change their availability. One of the reasons you may have been hired was because you could work, say, on Saturdays. If after a month, you suddenly cannot work on Saturdays anymore, there's a good chance your employer will tell you they no longer need you. You may be back to square one, looking for a job again. So, be accurate as to which days and times you are available to work.

The following chart can help you determine your availability. For example, if Jake gets out of school at 2 p.m., has basketball practice every Monday and Wednesday afternoons from 3 – 5 p.m., has to babysit his little brother every Saturday, and has to be home no later than 10:30 p.m., his availability worksheet would look like this:

Jake's availability worksheet

	Sunday	Monday	Tuesday	Wednesday	Thursday	Friday	Saturday
7 am		School	School	School	School	School	X
8 am		"	"	"	"	"	X
9 am		"	"	"	"	"	X
10 am		"	"	"	"	"	X
11 am	Open	"	"	"	"	"	Not
12 pm	anytime	"	"	"	"	"	available
1 pm	all day	"	"	"	"	"	anytime
2 pm	7 am–10 pm	School ends	School ends	School ends	School ends	School ends	Saturdays
3 pm		Basketball		Basketball			X
4 pm		till		till			X
5 pm		5 pm		5 pm			X
6 pm							X
7 pm							X
8 pm							X
9 pm							
10 pm							

This worksheet makes it easy to see when Jake is available to work.

On the application, Jake's availability would look like this (N/A means not available):

Sunday	Monday	Tuesday	Wednesday	Thursday	Friday	Saturday
anytime	6–10	3–10	6–10	3–10	3–10	N/A

> I had to give up basketball to get my job at the computer store. I couldn't do it all. I think I made the right choice.
>
> Shane, age 17.

When figuring out your availability, think about...

- Do you have a way to get to work?
- Do you have a way to get home?
- Do you have a curfew?
- If you're getting a ride, did you discuss it with that person?
- If you're borrowing the family car, did you discuss it with your parents or guardians?
- If you're using public transportation, do you know the bus/train schedule and whether it runs when you need it?
- How long will it take you to get ready for work?
- How long will it take you to get to work?
- Do you or will you have any sports activities?
- Are you now or will you be taking any classes?
- Do you have any religious commitments on certain days?
- Do you have any vacations planned?

Availability Worksheet

	Sunday	Monday	Tuesday	Wednesday	Thursday	Friday	Saturday
7 am							
8 am							
9 am							
10 am							
11 am							
12 pm							
1 pm							
2 pm							
3 pm							
4 pm							
5 pm							
6 pm							
7 pm							
8 pm							
9 pm							
10 pm							

This availability worksheet will help you figure out which days you can work and when.

Work experience: List the jobs you have had in the past, beginning with your most recent position. Fill this out **completely**. You might need to make some phone calls or look in the phone book to get the information. You will need to know the date you started and ended those jobs, your supervisors' names, the addresses and telephone numbers of the places of business, your job title and duties, your starting and ending salary and the reason for leaving.

There may be a section titled 'reason for leaving.' Do **not** leave this section blank. Be honest about why you left your last job and always try to turn it into something positive. *For example:*

terminated: to be let go from or fired from a job.

Dos and Don'ts...

Do write: "I was terminated because I was late too often, but I have learned from this experience and now I make sure I'm at work five minutes before I'm scheduled to work."
Don't write: "I got fired because I was late all the time"

Do write: "I want to work for a company that works as a team"
Don't write: "I didn't get along with my boss."

Do write: "I'm looking for a company with better opportunities."
Don't write: "I need more money."

Do write: "I needed more hours and they were only able to give me 10 hours a week."
Don't write: "I quit."

Do write: "I had a hard time getting to work but I am now applying to businesses within walking distance from my house."
Don't write: "Transportation problem."

Do write: "I had too many conflicts with school. I have learned to manage my time better and now I only work on weekends."
Don't write: "Left because of school."

Do write*:* "I had some family (or personal) problems that are now resolved."
Don't write: "Family problems." or "Personal problems."

May we contact your current employer?

If you are working and you do not want your current employer to know you are looking for another job, put "no." But if the reason you are leaving is because you need more hours or better pay, you might want to let your current employer know that. Maybe they cannot give you any more hours or they won't be able to give you a raise for another six months. If that's the case, they'll probably understand your desire to look for another job and appreciate that you let them know you are leaving. It will give them time to look for a replacement for you.

"I was scared to tell my boss that I was giving my two week notice. I thought he'd get mad. He didn't though. He asked if I was tired of taking orders and if I wanted to try making pizzas, instead. I got a raise, too.

Michelle, age 17.

References: A reference is an adult, other than a relative, who knows you well and can say what kind of worker you are. A reference is not a friend, a relative or previous employer that you have already listed on the application. It can be an adult friend of the family, a teacher, a coach, a neighbor or religious leader. You will need to call and ask if you can use them as a reference on your job application before you name them, though. A good reference can get you the job, so it is a good idea to be careful who you ask.

> *I put a friend of my Mom's down as a reference, but I didn't let her know. When they called her, she told them she had never heard of me . She couldn't think of any adults she knew named Monica. She felt really bad after she realized they were asking about me. I won't do that again.*
>
> Monica, age 18.

Education: Be specific and fill this out completely. List your high school(s) and college(s) with their addresses and the number of years you have completed. Make sure you include any additional training, such as computer classes, first aid training, swimming instruction, foreign language, etc.

Have you ever been convicted of a crime? It might also say "Have you ever been convicted of a felony?" They are asking if you have been convicted of more serious crimes here, such as murder, assault, battery or rape. This does not refer to parking tickets or other minor traffic offenses.

> **felony:** a serious crime that would send you to prison .
> **misdemeanor:** a less serious crime than a felony.

The open-ended question: This is a question that cannot be answered with a "yes" or "no." It is usually the last question on the application before your signature and will be worded in different ways:

- List any additional information you would like us to consider.
- Detail outstanding features of your last job.
- Why do you want to work for our company?
- What strengths would you bring to our company?
- Indicate any skills or experience which you believe reflect on your capability to perform...
- List any hobbies or special interests you have.
- Applicant comments.

They are all looking for the same thing. **They want to know something about you**. They want you to tell them something about yourself that will make them want to hire you. (They will also be looking to see if you can write a complete sentence.) Be truthful, enthusiastic, positive and brag about yourself. Tell them what you are and not what you aren't. Tell them what you have accomplished. Think of words that best describe you and use those, but be honest about yourself. Remember that the employer will probably check your references.

The following are some descriptive words you might use in answering the open-ended question. Use the ones that best describe who <u>you</u> are.

active	good natured	thorough	friendly
artistic	honest	ambitious	helpful
assertive	hard working	calm	handy
competent	on time	caring	mature
cooperative	patient	considerate	open minded
dependable	practical	creative	positive thinker
down-to-earth	reliable	detail oriented	resourceful
efficient	responsible	dynamic	sincere
enthusiastic	talented	energetic	team player
flexible	capable	fair	goal-oriented

When I applied at the grocery store, I wrote that I was a hard worker and dependable. I also wrote that I had handled money in my last job and dealt with customers. I think I got the job because I said I was dependable. People call in sick here all the time.

Eric, age 16.

Good Idea

> Don't forget jobs like babysitting, yard work, odd jobs, volunteer work and community service in this section. All that counts as work experience, too.

When you're done

Once you have completed the application and signed it, you may then take it back to the employer, following the same dress code you did when you obtained the application. The employer might want to do the interview when you return the application, so be prepared.

S.O.S. *Clothing Stores*

Please complete all requested information. Use ink and print.

GENERAL INFORMATION

LOCATION/STORE # CENTRAL MALL

TODAY'S DATE MARCH 3, 1997

NAME (LAST) WILLIAMS (FIRST) JACOB (MIDDLE) F.

SOCIAL SECURITY NUMBER 454-93-1020

STREET ADDRESS 101 SOUTH STREET

CITY SPRINGFIELD STATE CA ZIP 10001

TELEPHONE - HOME (333) 333-3333 TELEPHONE - WORK

IF YOU HAVE WORKED FOR OUR COMPANY BEFORE STATE WHERE, WHEN, FINAL POSITION, AND REASON FOR LEAVING:
NO

HAVE YOU EVER APPLIED TO OUR COMPANY BEFORE? IF YES, WHERE?
NO

POSITION DESIRED SALES

MINIMUM SALARY DESIRED $6.50/hour

DATE AVAILABLE FOR WORK JUNE 1

FULL TIME ☐ 30-40 HRS. PER WEEK   PART TIME ☒ 0-29 HRS. PER WEEK   SEASONAL ☐ HOLIDAY SUMMER

AGE: ARE YOU AT LEAST 18 YEARS OLD? YES ☒ NO ☐   IF YOU ARE UNDER 18, YOU MAY BE REQUIRED TO PROVIDE A WORK PERMIT PRIOR TO WORKING
ARE YOU AT LEAST 16 YEARS OLD? YES ☐ NO ☐

PLEASE INDICATE THE HOURS YOU ARE AVAILABLE TO WORK DURING BOTH DAY AND EVENING (i.e., 2 - 4 p.m., 6 - 10 p.m.)

SUNDAY	MONDAY	TUESDAY	WEDNESDAY	THURSDAY	FRIDAY	SATURDAY
1-5pm	5-9pm	5-9pm	5-9pm	—	—	9-5pm

NOTE: SHOULD YOUR AVAILABILITY CHANGE, IT IS YOUR RESPONSIBILITY TO NOTIFY YOUR SUPERVISOR.

DO YOU HAVE ANY RELATIVES NOW EMPLOYED BY OUR COMPANY? YES ☐ NO ☒
IF YES, IDENTIFY BY NAME(S), POSITION AND LOCATION:

WORK EXPERIENCE

LIST YOUR PREVIOUS EXPERIENCE BEGINNING WITH YOUR MOST RECENT POSITION:

1
EMPLOYER FRANKS DEPARTMENT STORE
ADDRESS STREET 100 MAIN STREET CITY SPRINGFIELD STATE CA ZIP 10001
PHONE (333)333-4000 SUPERVISOR BOB JONES NAME/TITLE STORE MGR.
REASON FOR LEAVING SEEKING SALES EXPERIENCE
STARTING POSITION LEAD CASHIER
LAST POSITION LEAD CASHIER
DUTIES DIRECT OTHER CASHIERS
STARTING SALARY $5.50/hour
FINAL SALARY $6.25/hour
DATES OF EMPLOYMENT START: MONTH JAN YEAR 1996 END: MONTH PRESENT YEAR

2
EMPLOYER WILLS FOOD STORE
ADDRESS STREET 250 WATER STREET CITY SPRINGFIELD STATE CA ZIP 10001
PHONE (333)333-4925 SUPERVISOR HARRY WHITE NAME/TITLE MGR.
REASON FOR LEAVING SEEKING GREATER RESPONSIBILITY
STARTING POSITION STOCK PERSON
LAST POSITION STOCK PERSON
DUTIES STOCK SHELVES. DID MONTHLY INVENTORY
STARTING SALARY $4.75/hour
FINAL SALARY $5.00/hour
DATES OF EMPLOYMENT START: MONTH FEB. YEAR 1994 END: MONTH JAN YEAR 1996

3
EMPLOYER
ADDRESS STREET CITY STATE ZIP
PHONE SUPERVISOR NAME/TITLE
REASON FOR LEAVING
STARTING POSITION
LAST POSITION
DUTIES
STARTING SALARY
FINAL SALARY
DATES OF EMPLOYMENT START: MONTH YEAR END: MONTH YEAR

MAY WE CONTACT YOUR CURRENT EMPLOYER? YES

REFERENCES

REFERENCE (NOT RELATED TO YOU) SUSAN SCHMIDT
ADDRESS STREET 120 MAIN ST. CITY SPRINGFIELD STATE CA ZIP 10001
PHONE (333) 333-1242 JOB TITLE LIBRARIAN
HOW ACQUAINTED AND FOR HOW LONG? DID VOLUNTEER WORK AT LIBRARY - 3 YEARS

REFERENCE (NOT RELATED TO YOU) HARVEY BROWN
ADDRESS STREET 182 SOUTH AVE CITY SPRINGFIELD STATE CA ZIP 10001
PHONE (333) 333-4010 JOB TITLE PERSONNEL MGR.
HOW ACQUAINTED AND FOR HOW LONG? EMPLOYED AT WILLS FOOD STORE - 2 YEARS

Sample Application: Always fill the application out completely and neatly!

EDUCATION AND TRAINING

SCHOOL	PLEASE PRINT NAME, STREET, CITY, STATE & ZIP CODE FOR EACH SCHOOL	NUMBER OF YEARS COMPLETED	DEGREE?	TYPE OF COURSE / MAJOR
COLLEGE	KANE COUNTY COLLEGE SPRINGFIELD, CA 10002	FRESHMAN	NO	COMMUNICATIONS
HIGH SCHOOL	DOUGLAS H.S., 200 MAIN, SPRINGFIELD, CA 10001	FOUR	YES	COLLEGE PREP.
ADDITIONAL TRAINING	YMCA, 300 WATER, SPRINGFIELD, CA 10001	ONE	NO	COMPUTER TRNG.

FOREIGN LANGUAGES __SPANISH__ SPOKEN FLUENTLY? __YES – 4 YEARS H.S.__

FOR OFFICE POSITIONS - INDICATE THE JOB SKILLS WHICH YOU HAVE PERFORMED:

☒ TYPING (__50-60__ WPM)   ☒ COMPUTERS/SOFTWARE __WORDPERFECT, WINDOWS 3.1, PHOTO SHOP__
☐ DICTAPHONE   ☐ 10-KEY BY TOUCH BY SIGHT
☒ OTHER: __CASH REGISTER__

ADDITIONAL EMPLOYMENT HISTORY INQUIRIES

HAVE YOU EVER BEEN DISMISSED OR FORCED TO RESIGN FROM ANY EMPLOYMENT?

☐ YES ☒ NO   IF YES, PLEASE EXPLAIN: _____

HAVE YOU BEEN CONVICTED OF A FELONY CRIME OR THEFT-RELATED MISDEMEANOR WITHIN THE LAST 5 YEARS?

☐ YES ☒ NO   IF YES, STATE DETAILS: _____
CONVICTIONS WILL NOT NECESSARILY DISQUALIFY APPLICANT; EACH CASE IS CONSIDERED INDIVIDUALLY.

PERMISSION TO WORK

IF EMPLOYMENT IS OFFERED, CAN YOU SUBMIT VERIFICATION OF YOUR LEGAL RIGHT TO WORK IN THE U.S.?
☒ YES   ☐ NO

REFERRAL SOURCE

☐ WALK-IN APPLICANT   ☒ NEWSPAPER AD   ☐ EMPLOYEE REFERRAL Name _____   ☐ OTHER (*please list*) _____

☐ COMMUNITY ORGANIZATION Name _____   ☐ SCHOOL/COLLEGE Name _____

WHY ARE YOU INTERESTED IN WORKING FOR OUR COMPANY?
__YOUR COMPANY HAS AN OUTSTANDING TRAINING PROGRAM FOR SALES PERSONS.__

WHAT STRENGTHS WOULD YOU BRING TO OUR COMPANY?
__I'M DEPENDABLE, HARD WORKING AND ENERGETIC. I SPEAK FLUENT SPANISH.__

WHAT DIDN'T YOU LIKE ABOUT YOUR PREVIOUS JOBS?   __LACK OF OPPORTUNITY FOR JOB GROWTH.__

APPLICANT'S STATEMENT

IF I AM EMPLOYED, I AGREE TO ABIDE BY THE RULES AND REGULATIONS OF THE COMPANY. I UNDERSTAND THAT MY EMPLOYMENT IS AT-WILL. THIS MEANS THAT I DO NOT HAVE A CONTRACT OF EMPLOYMENT FOR ANY PARTICULAR DURATION OR LIMITING THE GROUNDS FOR MY TERMINATION IN ANY WAY. I AM FREE TO RESIGN AT ANY TIME. SIMILARLY, S.O.S. IS FREE TO TERMINATE MY EMPLOYMENT AT ANY TIME FOR ANY REASON. I UNDERSTAND THAT WHILE PERSONNEL POLICIES, PROGRAMS AND PROCEDURES MAY EXIST AND BE CHANGED FROM TIME TO TIME, THE ONLY TIME MY AT-WILL STATUS COULD BE CHANGED IS IF I WERE TO ENTER INTO AN EXPRESS WRITTEN CONTRACT WITH S.O.S. EXPLICITLY PROMISING ME JOB SECURITY, CONTAINING THE WORDS "THIS IS AN EXPRESS CONTRACT OF EMPLOYMENT" AND SIGNED BY AN OFFICER OF S.O.S. THE ABOVE LANGUAGE CONTAINS OUR ENTIRE AGREEMENT ABOUT MY AT-WILL STATUS AND THERE ARE NO ORAL OR SIDE AGREEMENTS OF ANY KIND.

ALL OF THE INFORMATION I HAVE SUPPLIED IN THIS APPLICATION IS A TRUE AND COMPLETE STATEMENT OF THE FACTS, AND IF EMPLOYED, ANY FALSE STATEMENT OR OMISSION COULD RESULT IN IMMEDIATE DISMISSAL. I FURTHER AUTHORIZE YOU TO CONTACT ALL OF MY PREVIOUS EMPLOYERS OR REFERENCES FOR FULL INFORMATION REGARDING MY EMPLOYMENT HISTORY.

SIGNATURE __Jacob Williams__   DATE __March 3, 1997__

THIS APPLICATION WILL ONLY BE CONSIDERED FOR THREE MONTHS. IF YOU HAVE NOT BEEN HIRED WITHIN THREE MONTHS OF FILLING OUT THIS APPLICATION AND YOU WISH TO CONTINUE TO BE CONSIDERED FOR EMPLOYMENT, YOU MUST FILL OUT ANOTHER APPLICATION.

Getting Ready for the Interview

4

Tell anyone at your home who may answer the telephone that you have applied for jobs and you are expecting some phone calls. Ask them to take accurate messages for you and be certain to request the caller's name and telephone number. Keep a pen and paper near the phone.

When you answer the telephone, be certain to get the exact time, location and directions from the employer. Ask for the name of the person you should see.

Be on time

Estimate out how long it will take you to get to the interview. Think about traffic, the weather, the bus or train schedule and give yourself plenty of time. It's better to arrive 30 minutes early and kill some time before the interview, than to get there five minutes late. You probably won't get the job if you're late.

Check your attitude

Your nonverbal messages, (the way you dress, your eye contact, smiling, shaking hands, etc.) are just as important as what's on your application or what you will say during the interview. Even if you're shy, you can still make a great impression by just smiling and extending your hand when you first meet the interviewer. Introduce yourself. Chances are the employer has set up several interviews, so it's a good idea to identify yourself. Say, "Hi, my name is Josh and I'm here for an interview." This type of body language shows the employer that you are really interested in the job. You will not impress an employer if you are withdrawn and if you avoid eye contact.

Practice, practice, practice

The first thing you will do after introducing yourself to the employer is shake his or her hand. If you're not comfortable shaking hands, practice it with people you know. It's a friendly form of greeting and in business, people appreciate and expect it. A firm handshake shows that you are confident, professional and that you respect that person.

Practice good eye contact when others are talking to you, especially adults. Good eye contact shows that you are listening and that you care what the other person is saying. Think about times when you have talked to people and they did not have good eye contact with you. It probably felt like they weren't listening to you, even if they said they were. The employer will also feel like you aren't really listening if you don't have good eye contact. This doesn't mean you need to stare at that person. For example, you can look around the room or away when you're thinking of an answer to a question.

Do a practice interview with a friend, parent, teacher or someone who has been through an interview. Shake hands. Introduce yourself. Ask if you used good eye contact and if it seemed like you were really listening. You might feel silly doing this but you'll be more comfortable on the day of the actual interview because you'll have a better idea what to expect. It will help you loosen up. Have someone ask you questions that you think are likely to arise during an interview. (Examples are listed in the following chapter). Having your answers ready is much better than hesitating because you don't know what to say or you hadn't thought about the questions before.

> "I did practice interviews with my best friend, Dana, and some of the time we just laughed at each other. I think it did help, because she told me some of my answers were dumb. So, I had good answers ready for the interview."
>
> Katie, age 15.

What to wear

Your best bet is to dress conservatively, just as you dressed when you went to pick up the application. You don't need to wear a suit or a dress, but don't wear shorts or old jeans and a t-shirt. Pants and a button-down shirt are a safe bet, (girls could wear a skirt and stockings or tights instead of pants) and no hats. A tie is always a good idea. Wear nice shoes that are clean and shined instead of sandals or flip flops. This is your chance to make a good impression and the first thing the employer will notice is what you are wearing. Dress code is something you can discuss during the interview or after you are hired, but for the interview, look your best.

> "I wore one of my Mom's dresses to interview at a hospital. I really wanted that job and I wanted to look my best."
>
> Dana, age 18.

> "I wore khakis and a white button-down shirt to interview at a restaurant. I used to eat there a lot and noticed that was what the employees wore. So, I figured I'd fit in."
>
> Dan, age 17.

Little jewelry and natural looking makeup is advisable, too. It doesn't matter what the job is. Even if you'll be working outdoors wearing old t-shirts and worn jeans, look your best for the interview. Don't take any chances on not giving a good first impression.

Personal hygiene

You need to sell yourself so you must be presentable. This is your chance to convince an employer to hire you. It's like selling a bicycle. You'd want to clean it up, fill the tires and do any minor repairs to make it attractive to a buyer. You'd want the bike looking its best. Who would want to buy an old dirty bike with two flat tires?

The same applies when you're selling yourself. Put a little time and energy into looking your best. Sell yourself. Your hair should be clean, brushed and away from your face, and make sure you have showered or bathed on the day of the interview. Wear deodorant, too. Some people find perfumes offensive, so it's probably best not to wear any. Check out your nails and make sure they're clean. People notice hands. Remember to just look your best in any way you can. The employer will be checking you out from head to toe.

> **Personal Appearance Checklist:**
> ✔ Showered or bathed
> ✔ Hair washed and combed
> ✔ Deodorant on
> ✔ Nails clean. No chipped polish.
> ✔ Clothes clean and pressed
> ✔ Shoes clean and shined
> ✔ Little makeup or jewelry
> ✔ No perfume

Questions to ask

Think of questions *you* would like to ask during the interview. Even if you go into the interview with a piece of paper listing your questions, that's okay. In fact, that's probably a great idea because once you're in the interview, you might forget what you wanted to ask. It will also impress the employer that you have taken the time to develop a list. The following are some questions you might want to ask. In the next section to this chapter you will learn how to research a company, and you may wish to add more questions.

Who will be my immediate supervisor?

The person who interviews you may not be your supervisor. Some companies have recruiters or personnel departments that do all the hiring. Some businesspersons ask their assistants to help out in the interviewing process. It's a good idea to know who your boss will be and know his or her name.

For which days are you hiring?

The business may only need help on weekends. If you can work weekends now, but not after basketball season starts next month, you need to let the employer know. If you take the job for only one month, your employer may become frustrated if it will be necessary to hire and train someone new.

I need these days off. Would that be a problem?

Let the employer know ahead of time which days you cannot work. Maybe you have commitments on certain days of the week and won't be available. Maybe you visit your grandma every other weekend with the family. Don't keep this a secret until after you're hired. Let the employer know now.

Are you looking for morning, afternoon or evening help?

Again, if your availability will be changing in the near future, now is the time to let the employer know.

How long is a typical shift?

You need to think about your availability during the employer's regular shift. A typical shift may be from 3 p.m.- 9 p.m. If you don't get home from school until after 3 p.m., that could be a problem. Maybe the buses don't run on Sunday evenings and your shift ends at 9 p.m. You would have to make other transportation arrangements.

Is there a uniform or dress code?

This is important because you might have to buy special clothing. You'll want to consider how much it will cost to purchase, if it can be machine washed or if it needs to be dry cleaned. Dry cleaning can be expensive. If there are uniforms, how many will you get and will you have to buy them?

What is your policy on wearing jewelry, body piercings or tattoos?

You don't want to go to work on your first day and not know whether you should wear your hoop earrings or body piercings. Some businesses only allow minimal jewelry. If you have any doubts, check first.

For which positions are you hiring?

If you have applied at a local grocery store as a bagger and they're only hiring for help in the seafood department, you might not be interested in working there.

What skills are required to fill this position?

This question will give you a chance to see if your abilities match the job. What if they need someone who is very outgoing and talkative and not afraid to approach customers, but you're shy and uncomfortable doing that? Ask what your responsibilities will be.

What kind training will I receive?

Some businesses do training on the job (while you are working) and others have specific days or weeks when they do training. Find out in case you need to adjust your schedule during the training period.

How long does the training last?

If the training period lasts for two weeks, during a time when you usually aren't available, you will need to know that.

Will the rate of pay be the same during the training period?

Some companies pay a different rate while you are in training.

Will the training take place here or will I need to travel somewhere else?

Some companies do all their training at certain locations. Usually, they will reimburse you for travel expenses during this training period but be sure to ask that question if you have to travel.

Do you have an hourly rate of pay or do you pay a commission?

The company may pay you based on a commission, or a certain amount or percentage of your sales. However, most businesses pay an hourly rate.

Do you have other locations?

This question is important if you will be going away to college or moving to another area in the near future. You might want to transfer.

Do you offer medical and dental benefits for part-time or full-time help?

This question is important if you are not covered under your parents' medical or dental plans. Check with them first. If you are no longer a student or you are over the age of 18, you will want to learn about medical benefits.

Do you offer discounts for employees, vacation pay, holiday pay, sick days or retirement plans?

Some of these benefits are offered to full-time employees only. It's good to know, especially if you hope to become full-time in the future, and you are interviewing with two or three other businesses.

Do you offer scholarships or have a college tuition reimbursement program?

Some businesses offer this but it varies widely from company to company. If you're college bound, be sure to ask.

> *When I graduated from high school, the company I worked for offered me a manager trainee position. I wanted to go to college but I didn't know how I was going to afford it. My boss said the company offered a tuition reimbursement program to managers, so I could work full-time and take one or two classes a semester. I accepted and it's working great.*
>
> Sara, age 19.

Research the company

Knowing something about the company will impress the employer. You can find out some history on the company, financial information, who owns it, number of employees, and maybe even who you should contact when looking for a job. You can research a company in three ways: checking out the place of business in person, or at your local library, and on the Internet.

In person: Before you go for the interview, go to the place of business and look at how things are run, how many people are working, how they are dressed, what they are selling, and what the supervisor is doing. Be a customer. This can give you a lot of information and help you to ask important questions during the interview. For instance, you could bring up the dress code by saying, "I noticed all the employees wear jeans. What is your dress code?"

You could even ask the employees how they like their job when you go in as a customer. You could also ask your friends if they know anyone who works there and how they like it.

At the library and on the Internet: Libraries have a variety of resources to help you learn more about a business, and there is a lot of information available on the Internet. If you are still in school, your school library media center will have some reference books and electronic resources. Many schools also offer access to the Internet. Local public libraries are likely to have business directories and more specialized materials. A majority of public libraries also offer access to the Internet. Always remember to ask your school library media specialist or the reference librarian in a public library for assistance if you have difficulty locating or using any of these materials. They are there to help you.

Resources for Researching a Company

Compiled by Donna McMillen

To research a company, first check the most local resources, such as the telephone book, broaden your search to regional or state resources, then try for national resources and websites. In the phone book, you can find addresses, phone numbers, and advertisements that may give you clues about the business. Other local resources available at your library might include Contacts Influential or other business directories, addresses for local and state chambers of commerce, clipping files for articles on local businesses, collections of annual reports, a local online or CD-ROM newspaper index, phone disk or local magazines about the city or state.

Regional guides such as the JobBank series or the Insiders' Guide Series listed in chapter 1 should give information on local companies. Resources that cover the nation include:

Hoover's Handbook of American Companies

Moody's Guides

Ward's Business Directory of U.S. Private and Public Companies

The Million Dollar Directory

The National Directory of Addresses and Telephone Numbers

Standard and Poor's (multiple publications)

Thomas Register of Manufacturers

There are many others. You may also write or call the company to ask for any literature they can send you, such as an annual report. You can try the local office of the Small Business Administration (look in the federal government section of the telephone book.)

Print Resources

The Career Guide 1997: Dun's Employment Opportunities Directory. North America, Dun & Bradstreet Information Services, 1996. This is a directory of employers with more than 1000 employees, describing the company's activities, career opportunities, training and development, company locations, benefits, and contact address.

Peterson' Guides (Peterson's Job Opportunities in...) Princeton, NJ: Peterson's. These guides feature brief employer profiles along a few tips on researching a company. The series covers the fields of business, engineering and technology, health care, and the environment. Titles start: "Peterson's Job Opportunities in..."

Peterson's Hidden Job Market 1998: 2000 Companies That Are Hiring at Four Times the National Average. 7th ed. Princeton, NJ: Peterson's, 1997. This resource contains profiles of companies with name, address, website, when founded, number of employees, annual sales, annual increase in number of employees, and contact person.

CD-ROM and Online Databases

Check your local library to see if CD-ROM products for researching companies are available there. Examples are: American Business Disc, Dun's Million Dollar Disc, General BusinessFile, and others. Check also to see if they subscribe to online database search tools such as General BusinessFile, Magazine Index, National Newspaper Index or others. You can use these to search for magazine or newspaper articles, business reports and more. Find out what is available where you are.

Websites

Start your search with these library sites on how to research a company:

How to Find U. S. Company Information:
<http://www.nypl.org/research/sibl/company/companyinfo.html>. This is a guide to doing basic research on U.S. companies. The site includes links for company profiles and histories, financial information, current news, company websites, and further Internet resources gathered by the New York Public Library.

U.C. Berkeley Library Web: Berkeley Business Guides: No. 18: Internet Resources in Business & Economics: *<http:www.lib.berkeley.edu/BUSI/bbg18.html>*. This website offers recommended starting points and general reference sources as well as multiple links to specific business information.

Continue your search by trying the following websites:

The BigBook: *<http://www.bigbook.com>*.
This site offers information on over 11 million companies, searchable by name, location, and type of business. It includes directory information and a map.

Big Yellow: *<http://s16.bigyellow.com>*.
Over 16.5 million businesses are contained in these online yellow pages.

Commercial Services on the Net–Open Market: *<http://www.directory.net>*.
Searchable index of commercial websites for company home pages.

Companies Online: *<http://www.companiesonline.com>*.
Search for companies by name, location or industry to find ownership structure and links to company home pages.

Corporate Web Registry–Hoover's Company Profiles:
<http://www.hoovers.com/bizreg.html>.
Links to over 1,100 corporate websites.

EDGAR: *<http://www.sec.gov/edgarhp.htm>*.
Security Exchange Commission (SEC) filings for over 3,500 public corporations.

Hoover's Online: *<http://www.hoovers.com>*.
Using this database you can locate profiles for companies listed on the stock exchanges. This includes 1,200 private companies as well as links to other resources.

StreetLink: *<http://www.streetlink.com>*.
Quarterly reports from public companies.

Thomas Register of American Manufacturers: *<http://www.thomasregister.com>*.
Directory of American manufacturers.

Wall Street Research Net: *<http://www.wsrn.com/home/companyResearch.html>*.
Search by name or stock symbol to find links to company home pages, up-to-date stock quotes, SEC filings, press releases, company news and profiles.

Yahoo! Business and Economy: Companies:
<*http://www.yahoo.com/Business_and_Economy/Companies*>.
Company website links.

Yahoo! Business and Economy: Companies: Directories: Regional: U.S. States:
<*http://www.yahoo.com/Business_and_Economy/Companies/Directories/Regional/U_S_States*>.
Company website links by location.

How to Find Companies that offer Scholarships or Internships

Career Advisor Series. Detroit: Gale Research Inc. Gives general career information in a variety of fields including what companies look for in applicants, what is unique about the career, professional organizations, and listings for hundreds of companies with internship programs in each field. The series has titles for newspapers, magazine, book publishing, radio and television, marketing and sales, business and finance, healthcare, travel and hospitality, public relations, and advertising. A sample title is: Newspapers Career Directory (4th ed.) edited by Bradley J. Morgan, 1993.

Oldman, Mark and Samer Hamadeh. *Student Access Guide to America's Top Internships.* New York: Random House, Inc., 1995. Internship opportunities are listed alphabetically in entries containing information on the internship and how to apply, followed by indexes that list internships available to high school students, those that offer scholarships or free housing, which are most competitive, those available during the summer, and other categories such as location.

Peterson's Internships 1996: Over 35,000 Opportunities to Get Experience in Today's Competitive Job Market. 16th ed. Princeton, NJ: Peterson's, 1995. Listings of internship opportunities include general description, positions available, benefits, eligibility, and contact person. Indexes by field of interest and geographic area.

The Interview

5

Setting up a time

When employers are interested in talking to you about a job, they will call to set up a time for the interview. Check your schedule to be certain you can make it at the time you have both selected. One of the worst things you could do when going to an interview is be late, or worse, not show up at all. You probably won't get the job if you are late for an interview. The employer will assume that if you are late for the interview, you are likely to be late for work.

If you absolutely cannot make it to an interview at the scheduled time, call the employer as soon as possible, and not 10 minutes before your appointment. Your interview will probably be rescheduled for another day. Even if you have accepted a job and have an interview scheduled with a different employer, it will be appreciated if you call and cancel that interview. And if the first job doesn't work out, you might want to reapply for work at the other employer. If you don't show up for an interview without calling first, chances are very good that the interviewer will not reschedule your appointment, no matter what the excuse. You have only one chance to do it right.

Interview Checklist

✔ Pen with blue or black ink.

✔ Leave home so that you arrive a few minutes early.

✔ List of questions to ask the interviewer.

✔ Hours you are available to work.

✔ A date book or calendar.

✔ Any letters of recommendation.

✔ Resume, if you have one.

✔ Application, unless you have already returned it.

✔ Directions and telephone number in case you get lost.

✔ Appropriate dress and good personal hygiene.

✔ Attitude check.

Top 10 Things to Leave at Home

- Sunglasses
- Hats
- Body piercings/Too much jewelry
- Too much makeup
- Drinks
- Food
- Gum
- Beeper
- Cell phones
- Friends

Going in for the interview

You will probably be nervous the day of your interview, and that is perfectly normal. Even adults who have interviewed many times get a little tense. Take a few slow deep breaths, try to relax and remember to smile. Most interviews only last 15–20 minutes.

When you enter the place of business, introduce yourself and say that you are there for an interview. If you know who will interview you, ask for that person by name. For example, you might say, "Hi. My name is Jake and I have an interview with Sandy at 2 p.m."

When the interviewer approaches, smile, shake hands and introduce yourself. You will probably be taken to a place where you can talk privately.

When you are shown where to sit, take off your coat (if you are wearing one), put your belongings beside your chair and relax. Remember that the interviewer will want you to do most of the talking. Use good eye contact and answer all questions in full sentences. If there are two interviewers, talk to both of them, and not just one.

What's a group interview?

Some larger companies do group interviews. More than one applicant will be interviewed at the same time. Companies do this to weed out the applicants. This is your opportunity to stand out from the crowd. Don't be afraid to speak up and answer the interviewer's questions. Talk about yourself just as you would if you were being interviewed alone. Don't worry about the other applicants. They're nervous, too.

> *They did group interviews at the grocery store where I applied. It was like the first day of school where you go around and everybody takes turns telling about themselves. It was all right.*
>
> Mark, age 17.

Why a second interview?

You might be asked to come in for a second interview. That's a good sign. Some companies do second interviews to get an opinion from another management person, or it might be company policy. A business might also have someone from their personnel department do the first interview to screen out weak candidates. The second interview might be with a supervisor or manager.

> *At my first job interview, I was asked a lot of questions about school. I didn't have any job experience so I think the interviewer wanted to see if I was self-motivated. I think I got the job because I was relaxed and answered the questions well and gave examples.*
>
> Lyn, age 17.

Interview questions

The following is a list of questions many employers ask during an interview, with some examples on how to answer them. You won't necessarily be asked all of these questions, and these are not the only answers, but it's good practice and a good idea to have your own answer for all of them, just in case. Remember to relax, smile and look at the interviewer. Take your time answering the questions. Think about what you want to say. It's okay to pause and take a minute before answering, and remember to always be honest.

Dos and Don'ts...

Tell me about yourself.

This is a typical question that most employers use to start an interview. A good response is to ask whether there is any specific information they would like to know. Maybe they want to know about school, your plans for the future, what you do, what you are interested in, what activities you are involved in or what you have achieved in the past few years. When they tell you exactly what they want to know, brag about yourself. Talk about how well you have done in school, sports you enjoy, volunteer work, past jobs or awards you have won.

Do say: "Is there any specific information you want to know?" Once they answer, brag about yourself. "I'm a junior in high school and I play basketball. I'm a good swimmer. I'm on the swim team and occasionally I give private swimming lessons."

Don't say: "I was born in June in the year...."

Are you applying for other jobs?

If you're not, you should be. If this is the job you really want, tell them so.

Do say: "Yes, I've applied at several places but this one really appeals to me."

Don't say: "No, just here," or "yes."

Why should we hire you?

Tell them your strengths and what you have to offer. Maybe you're a dependable person, friendly, hard working, or have experience in this type of work.

Do say: "I'm a hard worker, and I do what's expected of me;" or "I would like to gain some experience in this field;" or "I've researched the company, and I appreciate the reputation it has earned. I think I'll fit in well."

Don't say: "I don't know."

How much money do you expect to make?

If you want more than minimum wage, know how much you want and be able to tell the interviewer why you are worth it.

Do say: "I would like to earn $5.75 an hour because I will need to use public transportation, and I have a year of experience in this field."

Don't say: "I don't know. Whatever you pay."

Have you ever handled money on the job?

Be honest, but turn it into something positive if you haven't previously handled cash.

Do say: "No, but I'm good at math, and I'm a fast learner;" or "Yes, I handled money and gave change in my last job. There was never a problem."

Don't say: "No," or "I don't like handling cash."

When are you available to work?

Don't say anything different than what you stated in your application. Know your availability. You don't want to say you can work anytime after school unless you're certain you can, especially if the business closes at midnight.

Do say: "I'm available to work these days and times..."

Don't say: "On my application I indicated I could work on Saturdays, but now I can't because...."

What are your plans for the future?

Even if you haven't decided what you're going to do with the rest of your life, tell the interviewer what you have been considering. The key is to talk about yourself. Do you plan to go to college? If so, where? What subjects do you want to study? Are you considering a technical school? If you're not planning to attend college, what do you think you'd like to do?

Do say: "I haven't decided yet, but if I don't go to college, I think I'll take some classes at a community college until I decide what I'd like to do."

Don't say: "I don't know yet."

What do you consider are your greatest strengths?

In other words, what do you do best? If you do well in math and science or computers in school, say so. Also, point out other strengths in your personality such as being hardworking, dependable, personable and good with people. Be prepared to give an example.

Do say: "I am very dependable. I'm never late for school or any appointment because other people count on you to be there when you're scheduled."

Don't say: "I don't know."

What are your weaknesses?

Answer this question with a positive response. What don't you do very well? Think about your personality. Are you a perfectionist? Do you need to accept that everything isn't going to be perfect all the time? Are you bad about picking up after yourself? Are your parents always after you to clean your room?

Do say: "I'm not very organized at times, but I'm changing that. I'm using a calendar to write down appointments. I'm keeping better track of my responsibilities."

Don't say: "I don't have any weaknesses."

What did you like about your previous job?

Did you like your boss? Did you like the people working there? Was it fun to work there? Did you like the hours?

Do say: "I learned a lot about working with a team and a diverse group of people."

Don't say: "The discount and the free food."

What didn't you like about your previous job?

Don't bad mouth your former employer. It makes you look bad.

Do say: "I wasn't challenged enough."

Don't say: "I didn't like my boss."

What qualities do you feel make a good supervisor?

Think about past supervisors, and what you liked about them. Were they fair? Could you talk to them about any kind of problem? Were they good teachers? If this is your first job, think about qualities you liked in teachers or other adults you have known. Did they listen well? Were they fair? Were they happy in their jobs?

Do say: "I like supervisors who are good teachers and fair to all employees."

Don't say: "They were friendly."

> *I said I respect someone like my Dad. He's patient and takes his time explaining things. I think someone like him would make a great supervisor.*
>
> Denise, age 18.

What motivates you?

What makes you want to do a good job at home or school? It's probably several things. Do you feel better about yourself when you do a good job? Do you set goals for yourself? Do you do better when goals are set for you?

Do say: "I always want to do my best," or "I set goals for myself."

Don't say: "Money."

When the pressure is on, where do you get extra energy?

Sometimes at work, you might be extremely busy or have a deadline to meet. The employer wants to know how you handle this kind of pressure. Think about deadlines on school projects or the pressure that comes with playing a sport or being on a team. How do you handle that kind of pressure?

Do say: "I set goals for myself. I do whatever it takes."

Don't say: "Caffeine."

Who is your mentor and why?

A mentor is a person you admire, and someone who gives you encouragement and sound advice. It could be a parent, a friend of one of your parents, a teacher, family member, or a religious leader. Be prepared to explain why you admire this person.

How do you handle disagreements with others?

Talking out problems with others rather than engaging in shouting matches or physical contact is the answer employers are seeking. Think about how you have handled conflict with members of your family, friends or previous employers. Think about times when you tried to resolve a conflict by talking with the other person, and be prepared to give an example.

How do you take criticism? Give me some examples.

Supervisors will be showing you how to do things in your new job. They will also be telling you what you do well and where you need to improve. Think about how you have reacted when a teacher or adult has said that you did something wrong and told you how to do it the correct way. How did you react?

Do say: "Once I thought I did really well on an English paper but I received a C. I was really disappointed but I talked to my teacher. He had some good points and showed me ways I could have done better." Another response might be to say "I'm a fast learner. I like to do a really good job, so I appreciate it when someone tries to help me."

Don't say: "Fine."

Why do you want to work for this company?

This is where your research on the company will help. Talk about what you found out about the company. Maybe you love shopping at their store. Perhaps, you applied at an amusement park because you're good with little kids, and you like working outside. Maybe you applied at their restaurant because it's close to home and you like their food. If you applied at a greenhouse, maybe it was because you love working with plants.

Do say: "I like your product," or "This is the field I want to study in college." Another approach would be to say "This company has a good reputation, and I'd be proud to work here."

Don't say: "I need a job."

When can you start?

The interviewer might ask if you can start next Wednesday. If you have a date book or calendar with you, it will permit you to answer right away instead of waiting until you get home to check your calendar.

Do you have any questions?

Never say no. The interviewer will probably think you aren't really interested in the job. Now is the time for you to take out your list of questions. *(See the sample questions in chapter 4.)* Don't be afraid to refer to it. The list will show that you are genuinely interested in the job. Employers appreciate it when applicants ask good questions.

The money question

Some employers will tell you during the interview how much the job pays. If it's not mentioned, only bring it up if you're offered the job on the spot. There is a right way to ask. Don't say: "What's the pay?" or "How much money will I make?" A better way is to say, "May I ask how much this job pays?" Otherwise, do not bring it up.

When employers decides to make a job offer, they will call and tell you what the job pays. You should have had an amount in mind when you submitted the application. If the amount is less than you expected, you will then need to decide if the money they are offering is acceptable. If not, be prepared to tell them why you are asking for more.

Ending the interview

When the interview has been completed, shake the interviewer's hand and thank him or her for the opportunity to apply. Ask, "When will you be making a decision?" or "When can I expect to hear from you?" The interviewer might tell you to call back in a few days, or notify you that a second interview will be scheduled. The interviewer may also explain that you will be called within a given period of time, perhaps a week or two.

After the interview, some companies do background checks, credit checks or drug testing.

> I was really nervous when I first went in to the interview, but the interviewer me told me that we went to the same grade school. She asked me if some of the teachers were still there and we talked about that for a little while. After a few minutes, I felt really comfortable talking to her and forgot that I was nervous.
>
> Mike, age 16.

Equal Employment Opportunity laws prohibit discrimination based on:

- age
- nationality
- ancestry
- religion
- marital status (if you're married or single)
- race
- color
- medical condition
- gender
- sexual orientation

Equal Employment Opportunity laws are in place to protect all citizens from discrimination. Be aware that discrimination based on any of the items in this list is against the law. For more information about the Equal Employment Opportunity laws and their enforcement see p. 60.

Follow up

You might want to send a thank you letter to the interviewer, expressing your appreciation for his or her time. Some employers interview up to 50 people a week, and they may not have the time to read 50 thank you notes. It's up to you. If you really want that particular job, and you think it would be a good move, go ahead and send one. A sample thank you note can be found at the end of this chapter.

If you don't hear from the interviewer by the end of the estimated time period, call the individual and ask if a decision has been made. Restate once again that you are interested in working at the company. When you call, ask for the person who interviewed you, then say, "Hi, my name is Jake Williams and I interviewed with you last week. I was wondering if you have selected someone for the job." If the interviewer says he or she needs more time and will call you back, say thank you and hang up. Never call back a second time unless it is specifically suggested.

If you are told that you didn't get the job, ask "For my future reference, what could I have done differently to improve my chances of getting a job?" The information could help you in your next interviews. Perhaps there were only three vacancies, but next month there might be twenty openings. In that case, ask how long your application will be kept on file. Remember to always be polite on the telephone. This could be a future employer.

Some companies send out rejection letters. These may state that they will not be offering you a job at this time, but they will keep your application on file for a given period of time. If you receive a rejection letter, do not call the interviewer. It doesn't mean that they will never offer you a job.

If the company offers to hire you, ask about the pay if you don't already know. Say, "May I ask what this job pays?" Then, ask when you are to start, where you are supposed to go, who to ask for and what you need to bring.

Jake Williams
101 South Street
Springfield, CA 10001
(333) 333-3333

Bob's Pizza Parlor
300 S. Main Street
Springfield, CA 10000

Dear Mr. Parker,

Thank you for taking the time to interview me last Tuesday. I would really like to work at Bob's Pizza and hope that you will consider me for a position there. I look forward to hearing from you.

Sincerely,

Jake Williams

Thank You letter: You can send a thank you letter to express your appreciation for being interviewed and to restate your interest in the job.

Congratulations, You Got the Job!

On your first day at work you will be asked to fill out several forms: an **Employment Eligibility Verification** (Federal form I-9, p. 46-47), a **Tax Withholding Statement** (Federal form W-4, p. 48), local or state tax forms, and possibly a few others, depending on the business. You might also want to fill out an **Earned Income Credit** form (Federal form W-5, p. 49–50) if you are a parent. Samples of these forms can be found at the end of this chapter.

The I-9 form proves that you have the right to work in the United States. A W-4 form tells your employer how much money to take out of your paycheck for taxes.

You will need to take some identification with you on your first day. A list of acceptable forms of identification can be found on the back of the I-9 form at the end of the chapter. Notice that you can take one document from List A *or* one from List B and one from List C. You may also need to take your work permit if you are under age. This can be obtained from your school. Your employer can tell you if a work permit is required, as this varies from state to state. If you will be working at a job where special certification is needed, (CPR, first aid, lifeguard, etc.) take that along on your first day, too.

Most places will ask for an emergency phone number. Have that number handy. It could be one of your parents' work numbers, or a neighbor or relative's telephone number.

> ### Start Your New Job on the Right Foot
> - Show up for work at least five minutes early.
> - Follow the rules and policies.
> - Take notes during your training.
> - Ask questions whenever instruction isn't clear.

What is direct deposit?

Many large corporations have direct deposit of wages. With direct deposit, your paycheck is deposited directly into your checking or savings account at your bank on pay day. What you will receive on pay day is a copy of your check so that you know how much was deposited into your account. The advantage is that you won't have to go into work every pay day to pick up your check, nor will you have to go to the bank to make a deposit. The money will already be there. However, if you don't already have a checking or savings account at a bank, you will need to open one. This is relatively easy, but you should call the bank you have selected and determine what identification will be required.

> *On the first day, a group of us watched videos on safety and customer service. Then, they paired us up with a head waiter or waitress and we followed them around and watched what they did. The rest of the week we were assigned to work with another waiter. After the second day, I waited on a couple of tables by myself. It wasn't as difficult as it looked. Just a lot to remember.*
>
> **Jack, age 18.**

What's a probationary period?

Many places of business put new employees on a 90 day probationary period. During this time, your supervisor will be watching to see if you are the right person for the job. The company might give you a different rate of pay during your probationary or training period. Ask your employer about that.

During your probationary period, ask your supervisor how you're doing and where improvements are needed. If during these 90 days the employer decides your work isn't satisfactory, your employment can be terminated. So, start out on the right foot and show them that you're a good employee.

Keeping your job

When employers look at applications, they do notice how long applicants stay with the same job. If an applicant has held several jobs in a short period of time, the employer will probably want to know why. They'll question whether or not it would be a good idea to hire someone who may only last a month or two. Keeping your job for a longer period shows that you are responsible and dependable.

Good Idea

Have other employees show you what they're doing and offer to help. They can teach you a lot.

Unfortunately, there's a high turnover rate in many jobs teenagers get. It's due to many different reasons, but short-term employment can be avoided if you go into a job knowing what is expected of you and what you can do to keep your job. The following are tips to help you keep your job and to show you what a business expects of their employees.

✔ Have a good attitude

This may sound vague, but having a good attitude means showing an interest in doing a good job. It also means that you have a willingness to learn, you're open to new ideas, and you can work well with others.

Employees with bad attitudes complain, they're unfriendly, and they don't work well with a team. They don't pitch in and help with duties. They grumble and have a tendency to look at the negative side of things. Employees with bad attitudes might be reluctant to wash dishes if they were hired as a cashier or sales clerk. They might grumble if their schedule is changed, instead of trying to work it out with the manager.

When you're hired for a job, realize that you will be asked to do whatever needs to be done, even if that includes washing dishes or cleaning up smelly garbage in the parking lot. This can happen with any job so you need to be flexible. If you start a job with an attitude that you weren't hired to clean windows or do any mopping, you need to realize there are few jobs where you don't have to do any dirty work. So, lend a hand and go in with the attitude that you'll do just about anything that's asked of you, within reason, of course.

Having a good attitude is probably the most important trait that employers value. When you have a good attitude, people like to work with you, they like to be around you, and they want you to be on their team.

✔ Be on time

Always show up to work a few minutes early. Give yourself time to put your belongings away and be ready to start work when you are scheduled.

If you're going to be late, call and let your supervisor know how late you will be. If you are ill, call your boss as soon as possible, preferably the day before or as soon as you know you won't be going to work. Your employer might need to get someone else to replace you, so give as much notice as possible.

Good Idea

Don't let a parent or a friend call in sick for you. Always call in yourself. The employer wants to hear from you.

✔ Follow the rules

Some companies will give you a training manual, have you watch a video or give you a list of policies and rules that must be followed. Read those. It usually includes things like dress code and appearance, clocking in and out, and how often you will be paid. You must follow all the rules in this manual, even if you get to work and see that other employees are not following them. For instance, if the manual states that jeans are not allowed and you see another employee wearing jeans to work, don't start wearing jeans. Ask and make sure it's okay, first. It could be that particular employee is on her way out the door because she isn't following the policy. So, don't assume anything. Always ask first.

"We had to buy our own uniforms. The cost was $40 for two shirts and a pair of shorts. They're real picky that your shirt has to be tucked in all the time, but they let us wear tennis shoes, and you can have long hair if it's pulled back. So, they're pretty cool."

Zachary, age 17.

✔ Stay busy

When you're at work and being paid for your time, give your employer 100 percent of yourself. If your friends stop by, tell them you can't talk when you're on the job. See them briefly when you go on break. Even chatting about your personal life with other co-workers can be a nuisance to your supervisor, and especially to customers. Think about times when you've been waiting for service at a store and the employees were busy talking with each other about what they did on Saturday night. Often customers who are ignored decide to shop somewhere else. So wait until you're on your own time to do your personal business.

If you find that you have nothing to do, ask your employer what else needs to be done. Stay busy. Look around and find something that needs to be cleaned, fixed, picked up or organized, without being asked to do it. It's called initiative. Remember that you're being paid to work.

For instance, if you've been hired as a receptionist to answer phones in an office, ask your supervisor what else you could be doing when the phones aren't busy. You could say, "Is there something else you would like me to do when the phones aren't ringing?" Show that you're ready to work. This isn't the time to pull out a magazine or catch up on your letter writing.

Good Idea

Don't use the phone at work for personal phone calls, unless there is an emergency. Always ask for your supervisor's permission before you use the phone.

✔ Volunteer

Take the initiative to volunteer for additional jobs, even the ones no one likes to do, such as taking the garbage out. It shows that you have a good attitude and are ready to work. When supervisors ask for help, don't hesitate to volunteer. When you see something that needs to be done, (mopping up a spill, cleaning under a table, cleaning the bathroom or the parking lot), volunteer to do it. For example, if they need people to stay late and help with inventory, offer to stay. You'll develop the reputation of being cooperative and a hard worker, and you'll be rewarded in time. It might not necessarily be in the form of a raise, but maybe you'll be the first to get the days off you requested, or maybe they'll give you the hours you requested on the next schedule. You'll be considered a good employee, and they'll want to keep you.

> *I think the most important thing is to get along with everyone at work and do your job well by doing more than is expected of you. Then everything else falls into place.*
>
> Melissa, age 16.

✔ Stay away from gossip

If you have a problem with a co-worker, your schedule, or anything else that is work related, talk to your boss about it. You might approach your supervisor by saying, "I need to talk to you privately about a problem I am having. When would you be available?" If you don't talk about your job-related problems with your boss, and try to solve them, it will only make the situation worse. Don't keep it inside and let it eat at you. It is equally bad if you talk about other people, complain about the schedule, and roll your eyes when you're asked to do something. You'll be perceived as someone with a bad attitude. If you're in a bad mood, make an effort to put that behind you while you're at work. Your employer is paying you to be happy and productive on the job.

Even if you don't like your supervisor, don't discuss that with other employees. It's okay if you don't like your supervisor. However, you do have to do your best to work with that person. You may not always like all of the other employees at your job, and that's okay. You're not there to make friends. Remember that your employer is a future job reference for you, so be professional and try to get along with everyone as best as you can.

When you're at work, never never never ...

... take a cell phone or beeper with you.

... discuss your salary with co-workers.

... criticize the supervisor.

... call in sick at the last minute.

... take any company property (including pens, paper clips, etc.).

... lie.

... abuse a discount or employee benefit.

... falsify hours worked.

... leave without giving a two week notice.

... be rude to or argue with customers.

U.S. Department of Justice
Immigration and Naturalization Service

OMB No. 1115-0136
Employment Eligibility Verification

Please read instructions carefully before completing this form. The instructions must be available during completion of this form. **ANTI-DISCRIMINATION NOTICE.** It is illegal to discriminate against work eligible individuals. Employers **CANNOT** specify which document(s) they will accept from an employee. The refusal to hire an individual because of a future expiration date may also constitute illegal discrimination.

Section 1. Employee Information and Verification. To be completed and signed by employee at the time employment begins

Print Name: Last	First	Middle Initial	Maiden Name
Address (Street Name and Number)		Apt. #	Date of Birth (month/day/year)
City	State	Zip Code	Social Security #

I am aware that federal law provides for imprisonment and/or fines for false statements or use of false documents in connection with the completion of this form.

I attest, under penalty of perjury, that I am (check one of the following):
☐ A citizen or national of the United States
☐ A Lawful Permanent Resident (Alien # A _____)
☐ An alien authorized to work until ____/____/____
(Alien # or Admission # _____)

Employee's Signature

Date (month/day/year)

Preparer and/or Translator Certification. (To be completed and signed if Section 1 is prepared by a person other than the employee.) I attest, under penalty of perjury, that I have assisted in the completion of this form and that to the best of my knowledge the information is true and correct.

Preparer's/Translator's Signature	Print Name
Address (Street Name and Number, City, State, Zip Code)	Date (month/day/year)

Section 2. Employer Review and Verification. To be completed and signed by employer. Examine one document from List A OR examine one document from List B **and** one from List C as listed on the reverse of this form and record the title, number and expiration date, if any, of the document(s)

	List A	OR	List B	AND	List C
Document title:					
Issuing authority:					
Document #:					
Expiration Date (if any):	___/___/___		___/___/___		___/___/___
Document #:					
Expiration Date (if any):	___/___/___				

CERTIFICATION - I attest, under penalty of perjury, that I have examined the document(s) presented by the above-named employee, that the above-listed document(s) appear to be genuine and to relate to the employee named, that the employee began employment on (month/day/year) ____/____/____ **and that to the best of my knowledge the employee is eligible to work in the United States.** (State employment agencies may omit the date the employee began employment).

Signature of Employer or Authorized Representative	Print Name	Title
Business or Organization Name	Address (Street Name and Number, City, State, Zip Code)	Date (month/day/year)

Section 3. Updating and Reverification. To be completed and signed by employer

A. New Name (if applicable)	B. Date of rehire (month/day/year) (if applicable)

C. If employee's previous grant of work authorization has expired, provide the information below for the document that establishes current employment eligibility.

Document Title: _____ Document #: _____ Expiration Date (if any): ___/___/___

I attest, under penalty of perjury, that to the best of my knowledge, this employee is eligible to work in the United States, and if the employee presented document(s), the document(s) I have examined appear to be genuine and to relate to the individual.

Signature of Employer or Authorized Representative	Date (month/day/year)

Form I-9 (Rev. 11-21-91) N

HR ADMINISTRATION

Employment Eligibility Verification (I-9): You will be asked to complete this form before you begin working. For more information the I-9 see p. 42.

LISTS OF ACCEPTABLE DOCUMENTS

LIST A		LIST B		LIST C
Documents that Establish Both Identity and Employment Eligibility	**OR**	**Documents that Establish Identity**	**AND**	**Documents that Establish Employment Eligibility**

LIST A — Documents that Establish Both Identity and Employment Eligibility

1. U.S. Passport (unexpired or expired)

2. Certificate of U.S. Citizenship (INS Form N-560 or N-561)

3. Certificate of Naturalization (INS Form N-550 or N-570)

4. Unexpired foreign passport, with I-551 stamp or attached INS Form I-94 indicating unexpired employment authorization

5. Alien Registration Receipt Card with photograph (INS Form I-151 or I-551)

6. Unexpired Temporary Resident Card (INS Form I-688)

7. Unexpired Employment Authorization Card (INS Form I-688A)

8. Unexpired Reentry Permit (INS Form I-327)

9. Unexpired Refugee Travel Document (INS Form I-571)

10. Unexpired Employment Authorization Document issued by the INS which contains a photograph (INS Form I-688B)

OR

LIST B — Documents that Establish Identity

1. Driver's license or ID card issued by a state or outlying possession of the United States provided it contains a photograph or information such as name, date of birth, sex, height, eye color, and address

2. ID card issued by federal, state, or local government agencies or entities provided it contains a photograph or information such as name, date of birth, sex, height, eye color, and address

3. School ID card with a photograph

4. Voter's registration card

5. U.S. Military card or draft record

6. Military dependent's ID card

7. U.S. Coast Guard Merchant Mariner Card

8. Native American tribal document

9. Driver's license issued by a Canadian government authority

For persons under age 18 who are unable to present a document listed above:

10. School record or report card

11. Clinic, doctor, or hospital record

12. Day-care or nursery school record

AND

LIST C — Documents that Establish Employment Eligibility

1. U.S. social security card issued by the Social Security Administration (other than a card stating it is not valid for employment)

2. Certification of Birth Abroad issued by the Department of State (Form FS-545 or Form DS-1350)

3. Original or certified copy of a birth certificate issued by a state, county, municipal authority or outlying possession of the United States bearing an official seal

4. Native American tribal document

5. U.S. Citizen ID Card (INS Form I-197)

6. ID Card for use of Resident Citizen in the United States (INS Form I-179)

7. Unexpired employment authorization document issued by the INS (other than those listed under List A)

Illustrations of many of these documents appear in Part 8 of the Handbook for Employers (M-274)

Form I-9 (Rev. 11-21-91) N

97910-3062
(Rev. 6/92)

Employment Eligibility Verification (I-9): This is the back side of the I-9. It lists documents that can be used to prove citizenship.. For more information the I-9 see p. 42.

Note: *You cannot claim exemption from withholding if (1) your income exceeds $650* dividends, you should consider making estimated tax payments using Form 1040-ES.

Sign This Form. Form W-4 is not considered valid unless you sign it.

Personal Allowances Worksheet

A Enter "1" for **yourself** if no one else can claim you as a dependent . . . . **A** _____

B Enter "1" if:
- You are single and have only one job; or
- You are married, have only one job, and your spouse does not work; or
- Your wages from a second job or your spouse's wages (or the total of both) are $1,000 or less.

. . **B** _____

C Enter "1" for your **spouse**. But, you may choose to enter -0- if you are married and have either a working spouse or more than one job (this may help you avoid having too little tax withheld) . . . . **C** _____

D Enter number of **dependents** (other than your spouse or yourself) you will claim on your tax return . . . . **D** _____

E Enter "1" if you will file as **head of household** on your tax return (see conditions under **Head of Household** above) . . **E** _____

F Enter "1" if you have at least $1,500 of **child or dependent care expenses** for which you plan to claim a credit . . **F** _____

G Add lines A through F and enter total here. **Note:** This amount may be different from the number of exemptions you claim on your return ▶ **G** _____

For accuracy, do all worksheets that apply.
- If you plan to **itemize or claim adjustments to income** and want to reduce your withholding, see the Deductions and Adjustments Worksheet on page 2.
- If you are **single** and have **more than one job** and your combined earnings from all jobs exceed $30,000 OR if you are **married** and have a **working spouse or more than one job,** and the combined earnings from all jobs exceed $50,000, see the Two-Earner/Two-Job Worksheet on page 2 if you want to avoid having too little tax withheld.
- If **neither** of the above situations applies, **stop here** and enter the number from line G on line 5 of Form W-4 below.

---- **Cut here and give the certificate to your employer. Keep the top portion for your records.** ----

Form **W-4**
Department of the Treasury
Internal Revenue Service

Employee's Withholding Allowance Certificate

▶ **For Privacy Act and Paperwork Reduction Act Notice, see reverse.**

OMB No. 1545-0010

1996

1 Type or print your first name and middle initial	Last name	2 Your social security number

Home address (number and street or rural route)	3 ☐ Single ☐ Married ☐ Married, but withhold at higher Single rate.
	Note: *If married, but legally separated, or spouse is a nonresident alien, check the Single box.*

City or town, state, and ZIP code	4 If your last name differs from that on your social security card, check here and call 1-800-772-1213 for a new card . . . . . ▶ ☐

5 Total number of allowances you are claiming (from line G above or from the worksheets on page 2 if they apply) . **5** _____

6 Additional amount, if any, you want withheld from each paycheck . . . . **6** $ _____

7 I claim exemption from withholding for 1996 and I certify that I meet **BOTH** of the following conditions for exemption:
- Last year I had a right to a refund of **ALL** Federal income tax withheld because I had **NO** tax liability; **AND**
- This year I expect a refund of **ALL** Federal income tax withheld because I expect to have **NO** tax liability.

If you meet both conditions, enter "EXEMPT" here . . . . ▶ **7** _____

Under penalties of perjury, I certify that I am entitled to the number of withholding allowances claimed on this certificate or entitled to claim exempt status.

Employee's signature ▶ _____ Date ▶ _____, 19 ___

8 Employer's name and address (Employer: Complete 8 and 10 only if sending to the IRS)	9 Office code (optional)	10 Employer identification number

Cat. No. 10220Q

Withholding Allowance (W-4)

The W-4 lets an employer know how much to withhold from each check for taxes. Make sure you ask your parents or employer any questions you have about this form. Don't wait till tax time!

Line A: Most teenagers have parents or guardians who claim them as dependents. Unless you support yourself, put "0" here.

Line B: Most teenagers claim "1" here. The more exemptions you claim, the more money you'll receive in each paycheck. However, you may end up owing money to the government at tax time.

Line C: This only pertains to you if you are married and want to claim your spouse. But, you may also claim "0" here.

Line D: This is for people who have children or other dependents that they claim on their tax return. For example, if you have two children, you may write in "2." You may also claim "0" even if you have dependents.

Line E: You may claim "1" here only if you support yourself.

Line F: You may claim "1" here if you have children and you pay more than $1500 in child care expenses yearly.

Line G: Add lines A through F. That total goes on line G. Most teens will have a total of "0." It's a good idea to discuss your exemptions with parents or guardians before you start your job.

19**97** Form W-5

Instructions

Purpose

Use Form W-5 if you are eligible to get part of the EIC in advance with your pay and choose to do so. The amount you can get in advance generally depends on your wages. If you are married, the amount of your advance EIC payments also depends on whether your spouse has filed a Form W-5 with his or her employer. However, your employer cannot give you more than $1,326 throughout 1997 with your pay.

If you do not choose to get advance payments, you can still claim the EIC on your 1997 tax return.

What Is the EIC?

The EIC is a credit for certain workers. It reduces tax you owe. It may give you a refund even if you don't owe any tax. For 1997, the EIC can be as much as $2,210 if you have one qualifying child; $3,656 if you have more than one qualifying child; $332 if you do not have a qualifying child. But you **cannot** get **advance** EIC payments unless you have a qualifying child. See **Who Is a Qualifying Child?** on this page.

Who Is Eligible To Get Advance EIC Payments?

You are eligible to get advance EIC payments if **all three** of the following apply.

1. You have at least one qualifying child.

2. You expect that your 1997 earned income and modified AGI (adjusted gross income) will each be less than $25,760. Include your spouse's income if you plan to file a joint return. As used on this form, earned income does not include amounts inmates in penal institutions are paid for their work. For most people, **modified AGI** is the same as adjusted gross income.

(You can look at page 1 of your 1996 tax return to find out what is included in adjusted gross income.) However, if you plan to file a 1997 Form 1040, see the 1996 Form 1040 instructions to figure your modified AGI.

3. You expect to be able to claim the EIC for 1997. To find out if you may be able to claim the EIC, answer the questions on page 2.

How Do I Get Advance EIC Payments?

If you are eligible to get advance EIC payments, fill in the Form W-5 at the bottom of this page. Then, detach it and give it to your employer. If you get advance payments, you **must** file a 1997 Federal income tax return.

You may have only **one** Form W-5 in effect with a current employer at one time. If you and your spouse are both employed, you should file separate Forms W-5.

This Form W-5 expires on December 31, 1997. If you are eligible to get advance EIC payments for 1998, you must file a new Form W-5 next year.

(TIP) *You may be able to get a larger credit when you file your 1997 return. For details, see* **Additional Credit** *on page 2.*

Who Is a Qualifying Child?

Any child who meets **all three** of the following conditions is a **qualifying child.**

1. The child is your son, daughter, adopted child, stepchild, foster child, or a descendant (for example, your grandchild) of your son, daughter, or adopted child.

Note: *An* **adopted child** *includes a child placed with you by an authorized placement agency for legal adoption even if the adoption is not final. A* **foster child** *is any child you cared for as your own child.*

2. The child is under age 19 at the end of 1997, or under age 24 at the end of 1997 and a full-time student, or any age at the end of 1997 and permanently and totally disabled.

3. The child lives with you in the United States for over half of 1997 (for all of 1997 if a foster child). If the child does not live with you for the required time because the child was born or died in 1997, the child is considered to have lived with you for all of 1997 if your home was the child's home for the entire time he or she was alive in 1997.

Note: *Temporary absences such as for school, medical care, or vacation count as time lived at home. Members of the military on extended active duty outside the United States are considered to be living in the United States.*

Married child.—If the child is married at the end of 1997, that child is a qualifying child only if you may claim him or her as your dependent, **or** the following **Exception** applies to you.

Exception. You are the custodial parent and would be able to claim the child as your dependent, but the noncustodial parent claims the child as a dependent because—

1. You signed **Form 8332,** Release of Claim to Exemption for Child of Divorced or Separated Parents, or a similar statement, agreeing not to claim the child for 1997, **or**

2. You have a pre-1985 divorce decree or separation agreement that allows the noncustodial parent to claim the child and he or she gives at least $600 for the child's support in 1997.

Qualifying child of more than one person.—If the child is a qualifying child of more than one person, only the person

(Continued on page 2)

▼ *Give the lower part to your employer; keep the top part for your records.* ▼

------- Detach here -------

Form **W-5**

Department of the Treasury
Internal Revenue Service

Earned Income Credit
Advance Payment Certificate

▶ **Give this certificate to your employer.**
▶ **This certificate expires on December 31, 1997.**

OMB No. 1545-1342

19**97**

Type or print your full name

Your social security number

Note: *If you get advance payments of the earned income credit for 1997, you* **must** *file a 1997 Federal income tax return. To get advance payments, you* **must** *have a qualifying child and your filing status must be any status* **except** *married filing a separate return.*

		Yes	No
1	I expect to be able to claim the earned income credit for 1997, I do not have another Form W-5 in effect with any other current employer, and I choose to get advance EIC payments.		
2	Do you have a qualifying child?		
3	Are you married?		
4	If you are married, does your spouse have a Form W-5 in effect for 1997 with any employer?		

Under penalties of perjury, I declare that the information I have furnished above is, to the best of my knowledge, true, correct, and complete.

Signature ▶

Date ▶

Earned Income Credit (W-5): This is a credit for workers with children and with income below set levels. To see if you qualify, read the eligibility requirements on this page and the following one.

Congratulations, You Got the Job!

Questions To See if You May Be Able To Claim the EIC for 1997

Caution: You **cannot** claim the EIC if you plan to file either **Form 2555** or **Form 2555-EZ** (relating to foreign earned income) for 1997. You also **cannot** claim the EIC if you are a nonresident alien for any part of 1997 unless you are married to a U.S. citizen or resident and elect to be taxed as a resident alien for all of 1997.

1 Do you have a qualifying child? Read **Who Is a Qualifying Child?** on page 1 before you answer this question. If the child is married, be sure you also read **Married child** on page 1.

☐ **No. Stop.** You may be able to claim the EIC but you **cannot** get advance EIC payments.

☐ **Yes.** Go to question 2.

Caution: If the child is a qualifying child for both you and another person, the child is your qualifying child only if you expect your 1997 modified AGI to be **higher** than the other person's modified AGI. If the other person is your spouse and you expect to file a joint return for 1997, this rule does not apply.

2 Do you expect your 1997 filing status to be Married filing a separate return?

☐ **Yes. Stop.** You **cannot** claim the EIC.

☐ **No.** Go to question 3.

(TIP) If you expect to file a joint return for 1997, include your spouse's income when answering questions 3 and 4.

3 Do you expect that your 1997 earned income and modified AGI (see page 1) will each be less than $25,760 (less than $29,290 if you have more than one qualifying child)?

☐ **No. Stop.** You **cannot** claim the EIC.

☐ **Yes.** Go to question 4. But remember, you **cannot** get advance EIC payments if you think your 1997 earned income or modified AGI will be $25,760 or more.

4 Do you expect that your 1997 investment income will be more than $2,250? For most people, investment income is the total of their taxable interest and dividends and tax-exempt interest. However, if you plan to file a 1997 Form 1040, see the 1996 Form 1040 instructions to figure your investment income.

☐ **Yes. Stop.** You **cannot** claim the EIC.

☐ **No.** Go to question 5.

5 Do you expect that you (or your spouse if filing a joint return) will be a qualifying child of another person for 1997?

☐ **No.** You may be able to claim the EIC.

☐ **Yes.** You **cannot** claim the EIC.

---

with the **highest** modified AGI for 1997 may treat that child as a qualifying child. If the other person is your spouse and you plan to file a joint return for 1997, this rule does not apply.

Reminder.—Your qualifying child must have a social security number.

What If My Situation Changes?

If your situation changes after you give Form W-5 to your employer, you will probably need to file a new Form W-5. For example, you should file a new Form W-5 if any of the following applies for 1997.

● You no longer have a qualifying child. Check **"No"** on line 2 of your new Form W-5.

● You no longer expect to be able to claim the EIC for 1997. Check **"No"** on line 1 of your new Form W-5.

● You no longer want advance payments. Check **"No"** on line 1 of your new Form W-5.

● Your spouse files Form W-5 with his or her employer. Check **"Yes"** on line 4 of your new Form W-5.

Note: If you get the EIC with your pay and find you are not eligible, you must pay it back when you file your 1997 Federal income tax return.

Additional Information

How To Claim the EIC

If you are eligible, claim the EIC on your 1997 tax return. See your 1997 instruction booklet.

Additional Credit

You may be able to claim a larger credit when you file your 1997 tax return because your employer cannot give you more than $1,326 of the EIC throughout the year with your pay. You may also be able to claim a larger credit if you have more than one qualifying child. But you must file your 1997 tax return to claim any additional credit.

Privacy Act and Paperwork Reduction Act Notice

We ask for the information on this form to carry out the Internal Revenue laws of the United States. Internal Revenue Code sections 3507 and 6109 and their regulations require you to provide the information requested on Form W-5 and give the form to your employer if you want advance payment of the EIC. As provided by law, we may give the information to the Department of Justice and other Federal

agencies. In addition, we may give it to cities, states, and the District of Columbia so they may carry out their tax laws.

You are not required to provide the information requested on a form that is subject to the Paperwork Reduction Act unless the form displays a valid OMB control number. Books or records relating to a form or its instructions must be retained as long as their contents may become material in the administration of any Internal Revenue law. Generally, tax returns and return information are confidential, as required by Code section 6103.

The time needed to complete this form will vary depending on individual circumstances. The estimated average time is: **Recordkeeping,** 7 min.; **Learning about the law or the form,** 9 min.; and **Preparing the form,** 27 min.

If you have comments concerning the accuracy of these time estimates or suggestions for making this form simpler, we would be happy to hear from you. You can write to the Tax Forms Committee, Western Area Distribution Center, Rancho Cordova, CA 95743-0001. **DO NOT** send the form to this address. Instead, give it to your employer.

(♻) *Printed on recycled paper*

*U.S. Government Printing Office: 1996 — 407-124

Earned Income Credit (W-5), second page: See p. 49 for the rest of the document. See p. 42 for more information about the forms in this section.

Time to Say Goodbye

It's preferable to try and stay in your present job whenever possible. If you have a problem, your employer might be able to help by reducing your hours, changing your schedule, or transferring you to a different location, depending on your needs. For example, if you're considering quitting because school is starting, maybe your hours can be changed to weekends or one or two afternoons a week. It's always worth keeping a good job, so give it a try. If you job hop, future employers might not want to take a chance hiring you.

The following are some reasons you may want to leave your job, along with possible solutions to help you consider all options before resigning.

Problem: You don't get along with co-workers.

Solution: Try to determine what the problem is. Do co-workers give you the cold shoulder? Maybe they feel you don't carry your weight at work, and they end up doing your job. Is the problem with one or two people? Maybe there's a personality conflict, and you both just need to adjust and get along as well as possible. Are some of the other employees goofing off, requiring you to work harder? The supervisors may already know who the goof-offs are, but if it becomes a problem for you, try talking to your manager about it.

Unless you are being verbally or physically abused or discriminated against, you shouldn't leave your job just because you aren't getting along with others. There may always be people at work who you don't like, no matter where you go. So don't run away from the problem.

Communication is the key here, but don't walk up to a co-worker and say "Do you have a problem with me?" They'll probably say "No," and you will have accomplished nothing. Try approaching your co-worker by asking a question about work or how to do a certain job. After you have talked to the person about other things for a while, you could say, "You seemed a little upset with me yesterday. Did I do something wrong?"

If that doesn't work and the problem continues, or if the problem is really something that your supervisor should address, talk to your supervisor about it. You don't want to tattle, so you could say, "It seems like Jason and I don't get along well at work. I'd like to resolve this problem. What do you think I should do?" Managers have a lot of experience dealing with people problems, and your boss will be able to give you some good advice.

> "I didn't get along with this one girl at work when I first started. I decided to ask for her help on a project I was supposed to do. She had been there over a year and knew exactly how it was supposed to be done. She taught me a lot that day, and since then we've worked well together. The tension has gone."
>
> Shannon, age 18.

If you leave a job every time you don't get along with someone, you'll be looking for a new job every few weeks. It'll be harder to find a new job each time, because employers don't want to hire someone who doesn't get along with other people.

Problem: You don't like your boss.
Solution: You won't always like your boss in every work situation, and that's okay. Your boss is not there to be your friend. Put yourself in the supervisor's shoes and realize there is a job to be done, and getting it done well is what matters. Try to get along with your boss as best as possible, or look into a transfer before resigning.

Problem: Your job is interfering with your school work and your grades are slipping.
Solution: Your grades are very important, but before you throw in the towel and leave your job, try to organize your time better. Use study halls to do homework. Try blocking out a certain time of day, such as 3:00 - 4:30 p.m. every day for studying, and stick to it. Ask friends not to call, or turn the answering machine on during those times. Try cutting back on your social life and the time you spend on the telephone with friends. Ask your supervisor if your hours could be reduced to give you more study time.

I had to cut my hours way back because of my grades. I wanted to make the same money I made in the summer, but it wasn't working out.

Ryan, age 16.

Problem: Your availability has changed.
Solution: Talk to your supervisor as soon as you know you need to change your schedule. Your boss may not be able to accommodate you, but if you give early notice, there is a greater possibility something can be worked out. However, you need to understand that if your new schedule doesn't meet the needs of the business, you will probably lose your job.

Problem: You were given a written or verbal warning.
Solution: If you think you were unfairly criticized, speak to your supervisor about it. Don't let it eat at you for three weeks and then leave your job. If you did something wrong and the criticism was justified, look at it as a learning experience. For example, if you were written up for getting to work late, make it a point to arrive ten minutes early every day. This shows that you are mature and can handle criticism well.

Problem: You have been offered another job with more money.
Solution: First of all, consider several other things besides the money. Will you have to travel further? Is the other employer offering you more or fewer hours? Do you think you'd

I got a verbal warning for getting too many personal phone calls. I was embarrassed about it, but I didn't blame the manager at all. I told my friends I'd lose my job if they didn't quit calling me at work. That's worked so far.

Brandon, age 17.

like to work for that company more than your present employer? How long will your training last? What will your job be?

If after answering these questions you are still considering the other job, have a talk with your present supervisor. Tell him or her that you have been offered another job with more pay. If you're valuable to your employer, and the company can afford it, you might be offered more money to stay. It's worth a shot.

Problem: You want to work at the same business where some of your friends are working.

Solution: Again, consider how far you will need to travel, the pay, the nature of the job, and the number of hours you would work at this other job. Also, consider that you might be assigned to a different area or have different hours and may never see your friends.

Problem: You're moving or going away to school.

Solution: Check into a transfer to another location within the same company if you're working for a large corporation. You've already been trained, so it's usually easy to get a transfer. If you're not working for a large company or they have no other employment opportunities where you will be moving, ask if you could be considered for summer or holiday employment, if you'll be returning to the community during those times.

Problem: Your work environment is unsafe.

Solution: Tell your supervisor about the unsafe situation immediately. If that doesn't work, talk with an adult about the hazard. If they agree that it is serious, call the Occupational Safety and Health Administration (OSHA), which is a federal agency with offices in many locations. Their phone number is listed in the government section of your phone book.

Problem: You're bored and want to do something new.

Solution: Communication is the key. Talk to your supervisor before you give your two week notice. Tell your boss that you want to learn something new. Find out if there is another job you could learn or if you could be given additional responsibilities. Your supervisor won't know that you're interested in doing something else unless you discuss it.

"I asked if I could do something besides stocking books every day, so they taught me how to run the registers and work in the music department. There was a lot to learn but my job is more interesting."

Nicky, age 17.

Problem: Your boss is lewd, rude and crude.

Solution: If at any time you feel you are being mentally, physically or sexually harassed or discriminated against by a supervisor, talk to an adult about it so action can be taken. You could also get in touch with your supervisor's boss or call the Department of Labor (See the government section of your telephone book.)

Problem: Your employment was terminated.

Solution: If the reason for the termination is due to a reduction in staff, there's nothing you can do about that except to ask for a letter of recommendation. If you were terminated because you broke company policy, look at it as a learning experience and plan to do things differently in your next job.

Two weeks notice

When it's time to leave your job, always give at least a two weeks notice to your employer, preferably in writing. A sample letter of resignation is included at the end of this chapter. Your supervisor will need to know you will be quitting at least two weeks before your last day. This will give the company an opportunity to find a replacement. You want to leave on good terms with your employer so your supervisor will give you a good recommendation in the future. Remember that your previous employers become your future job references, so work hard through your last day. Even if you have been an excellent employee, if your job performance is poor during those last two weeks, that will be what your supervisor remembers.

Good Idea

> Determine if you can afford to leave your present job before you have another one lined up. You never know how long it will take to get another job.

What about my last paycheck?

Ask your employer how to get your last paycheck. You will also need to leave a forwarding address if you're moving, so you can receive your W-2 form (report of your tax withholdings) at tax time.

Letter of recommendation

Before you leave, ask your employer for a letter of recommendation to take with you, especially if you are moving away.

**Good Idea**

> Make several copies of your letter(s) of recommendation. Employers sometimes like to keep them with your file.

Jake Williams
101 South Street
Springfield, CA 10001
(333) 333-3333

Bob's Pizza Parlor
300 S. Main Street
Springfield, CA 10000

Dear Mr. Parker:

This is to inform you that I will be moving to Illinois to start college in a few weeks and my last day of work will be on Friday, August 17. I have really enjoyed working for you this summer. I would appreciate being considered for a job next summer, when I will be returning to Springfield.

Sincerely,
Jake Williams

Letter of resignation: Give your employer a letter of resignation at least two weeks before you plan to leave.

On your mark, get set...

Knowing and using the basic tools in this book can give you a big advantage over other candidates applying for the same job, even if they have years of experience, more education and a better resume. They could be passed over for a job simply because they didn't dress appropriately or use good eye contact during the interview. On the other hand, you might get the job because the interviewer was impressed with research you did on the company or the list of questions you prepared about the job. These are things that count.

These basic job skills will not only help you get a job as a teenager, but also as an adult in any occupation. **You have the tools, now it's up to you!**

... Go

Resources on Employment-Related Topics

Selecting a Career

Bolles, Richard Nelson. *What Color Is Your Parachute?: A Practical Manual for Job-Hunters and Career-Changers.* Berkeley, CA: Ten Speed, 1997. Perennial favorite includes most effective and least effective job-hunting methods, how to choose a career, finding the person who has the power to hire you, conducting the interview and finding a mission in life. Includes a chapter on job hunting for high school students and for summer jobs.

Klein, Laura, Marisa Cohen, and Rory Evans. "Summer Jobs: Work It Girl." (includes related articles) *Seventeen*, May 1994, v53 n5 p74+. Rating of summer jobs by pay and experience, interviews with an MTV intern, a political intern, and a day camp entrepreneur.

Krannich, Ronald L. and Caryl Rae Krannich. *The Best Jobs for the 1990s and Into the 21st Century.* 2nd ed. Manassas Park, VA: Impact, 1995. Lists of the current top careers, best choices for future careers, trends and new technologies, best places to live, brief information on the top careers, extensive list of further resources including electronic sources.

Mannarino, Melanie, and others. "No-Bummer Summer: On a Roll." *Seventeen*, May 1997 v56 n5 p110+. Includes information on internships, volunteer numbers, interviews with workers from a national park, a theme park, and McDonalds.

Maze, Marilyn and Donald Mayall. *The Enhanced Guide for Occupational Exploration: Descriptions for the 2,800 Most Important Jobs.* 2nd ed., revised. Indianapolis, IN: JIST Works, 1995. "Based on information from the U.S. Department of Labor and Other Sources," this volume contains job descriptions with codes for salary range, environmental factors, physical demands, noise levels, outlook, aptitudes, and education needed.

Occupational Outlook Handbook. 1996-97 ed. U.S. Department of Labor, Bureau of Labor Statistics. 1996. Standard source for career exploration. Gives career descriptions, working conditions, employment opportunities, training and qualifications, advancement possibilities, job outlook, earnings, related occupations, and sources of additional information.

Wright, John W. *The American Almanac of Jobs and Salaries.* New York: Avon, 1996. Average salaries in a wide variety of career fields.

Websites

Career, College & Business Resources from the Chico High School Library: <http://www.chs.chico.k12.ca.us/libr/webres/career.html>. Extensive bibliography of resources for employment, college, and financial aid.

IPL: the Internet Public Library: Teen Division: <http://www.ipl.org/teen/>. Check this site for teens under Career and College for links to college choice and planning for the future.

Kids & Jobs: <http://www.pbs.org/jobs/>. Public television site for teens, parents and educators on career exploration.

What Color is Your Parachute: Job Hunting Online: <washingtonpost.com/parachute/>. The Net Guide includes links to jobs, resumes, counseling, networking and research and is based on a chapter from Richard Bolles' book.

Career Exploration Series

Beckett, Kathleen. *Fashion.* Princeton, NJ: Peterson's, 1992. This title from the Careers Without College series covers information on careers within the field of fashion and includes further educational resources. Other books in the series cover careers with cars, computers, fitness, health care, and music.

Camenson, Blythe. *Careers for Health Nuts and Others Who Like to Stay Fit.* Lincolnwood, IL: NTC/Contemporary, 1996. This cleverly titled series gives information on careers within a field, including associations, training programs, further reading, some employer addresses, personal experiences, and an aptitude questionnaire for each area. Other books in the series are aimed at gourmets, travel buffs, fashion plates, self-starters, sports nuts, lovers of nature, art, animals or culture, car or film or mystery buffs, crafty people, good samaritans and others. Titles start "Careers for..." and are part of this VGM Careers for You series.

Camenson, Blythe. *Great Jobs for Art Majors.* Lincolnwood, IL: NTC/Contemporary, 1997. The books in this series give information on networking, job search, resumes, interviews, career paths, graduate education and additional resources for career areas including business, communications, engineering, English, foreign language, liberal arts, psychology, and sociology. Series titles begin "Great Jobs for...."

Career Associates. *Career Choices for Students of History.* New York: Walker, 1990. Vocational guidance includes outline of job, qualifications, job outlook, major employers, and resources. Other books in the series cover art, business, communications, computer science, economics, English, mathematics, and psychology. Titles start: "Career Choices for the 90's: For Students of..."

Eberts, Marjorie, Linda Brothers, and Ann Gisler. *Careers in Travel, Tourism, and Hospitality.* Lincolnwood, IL: NTC, 1997. Entries in the series explore careers with information on settings, working conditions, preparation and training requirements, aptitudes, advancement, salary, fringe benefits and rewards, typical day, and a personal narrative from someone in that career. Appendices list schools and colleges. The series covers careers in computers, international business, medicine, science, law, communications, education, advertising, and many more. Titles start "Careers in..." and are by various authors.

Field, Shelly. *Career Opportunities in the Sports Industry.* New York: Facts on File, 1991. Profiles of careers include the career ladder, duties, salary range, employment prospects, geographical locations, prerequisites, position description, unions/associations, tips on entry, and appendices for educational institutions, major employers, associations, and additional resources. Other books in the series profile opportunities in art, theater and performing arts, travel and tourism, music industry, television and video, or food and beverage.

Krannich, Ronald L. and Caryl Rae Krannich. *Jobs for People Who Love Travel: Opportunities at Home and Abroad.* 2nd ed. Manassas Park, VA: Impact, 1995. Breaks down career areas to highlight job possibilities including internships and volunteerism. Includes aptitude test, further resources and government opportunities. Other books by the same authors are for people who love computers, health care, resorts or cruise ships, or working from home.

Paradis, Adrian A. *Opportunities in Part-time and Summer Jobs.* Lincolnwood, IL: NTC/Contemporary, 1997. Ideas for part-time and summer employment, with brief descriptions of a variety of jobs perfect for teens, including ideas for operating your own business such as lawn care or pet care. Also includes budgeting, job hunting, and how to succeed in your job. Other books in the series cover career fields such as marine science, paramedical and business. Titles start "Opportunities in..." and are by various authors.

Peterson's Job Opportunities in the Environment 1995. Princeton, NJ: Peterson's, 1994. This guide features job hunting tips, brief employer profiles, some in-depth company profiles, seeking employment with smaller rapid-growth companies, and tips on researching a company. The series covers the fields of business, engineering, technology, and health care. Titles start: "Peterson's Job Opportunities in..."

Resumes and Cover Letters

Adams Cover Letter Almanac and Disk. Holbrook, MA: Adams Media, 1996. How to write a cover letter and hundreds of sample letters including cover letters, rejection or acceptance letters, thank-you letters, networking letters and others. Software disk for Adams FastLetter included.

Adams Resume Almanac and Disk. Holbrook, MA: Adams Media, 1996. Hundreds of sample cover letters, including selections for students. Software disk for Adams FastResume included.

Reed, Jean. *Resumes That Get Jobs.* 8th ed. New York: Macmillan, 1995. Contains tips on preparing resumes and cover letters, sample resumes, strategic marketing, and suggested reading.

Gonyea, James C. and Wayne M. Gonyea. *Electronic Resumes: A Complete Guide to Putting Your Resume On-line.* New York: McGraw-Hill, 1996. Includes a Windows software disk with Resume Online and Resumaker. The book/disk combination includes tips on the advantages of an electronic resume, how to create a multimedia resume, precautions to keep in mind, and how to create an electronic resume.

Resumes for High School Graduates. Lincolnwood, Il: VGM Career Horizons, 1993. Basics for new graduates; includes numerous sample resumes and cover letters.

Rosenberg, Arthur D. and David Hizer. *The Resume Handbook: How to Write Outstanding Resumes and Cover Letters for Every Situation.* 3rd ed. Holbrook, MA: Adams Media, 1996. Basic and helpful resume guide includes both good and bad resume examples.

Interview Guides

Adams Job Interview Almanac. Holbrook, MA: Adams Media, 1996. 1800 interview questions with answers and tips on answering for both general interviews and for specific careers.

Barton, Jim. *Jim Barton's The Job Interview and You!* Montvale, NJ: Career Path Productions, 1992. (videorecording, one hour) Barton presents a seven step plan for preparing for an interview with tips for everyone from entry level to management.

Bloch, Deborah P. *How to Get and Get Ahead on Your First Job.* Lincolnwood, IL: NTC, 1993. Offers basic information on where to look for jobs, applications, resumes, interviews, on-the-job success, and moving up or on.

Fry, Ron. *Your First Job: for College Students—and Anyone Preparing to Enter Today's Tough Job Market.* Hawthorne, NJ: Career Press, 1993. Humorous, brief chapters on the basics of finding, landing, and keeping a job, including resume and interview tips.

Medley, H. Anthony. *Sweaty Palms: The Neglected Art of Being Interviewed.* Berkeley, CA: Ten Speed, 1992. Sought after guide covers the basics of interviewing—what to expect, how to prepare and how to project a confident manner. Includes information on types of interviews, dress, salary, evaluation factors, and commonly asked questions.

Managing School/Work Responsibilities

Bensimhon, Miriam and Andy Levin. "The Exhausting Days and Sleepless Nights of a Working Teenager." *Life*, July 1993 v16 n8 p74+. A teen's grades are affected by her work schedule, threatening her chances of getting into the college she wants.

Crispell, Diane. "Why Working Teens Get Into Trouble." *American Demographics,* Feb 1997 v17 n2 p19+. Research shows working teens may have lowered grades, increased behavioral and health problems, and likelihood of drug abuse as they work more hours.

Jacob, Rahul. "Too Much Work = Poor Grades." *Fortune*, April 5, 1993 v 127 n7 p92. Extra hours on homework may offer a better long-term benefit than increased work hours for students.

"Mixing Work and High School." *Good Housekeeping*, Oct 1993 v217 n4 p192. Balancing work with homework.

Saltzman, Amy. "Mom, Dad, I Want a Job." *U.S. News & World Report*, May 17, 1993 v 114 n19 p68+. Four teens profiles show negatives may outweigh positives if teens work more than 20 hours a week—lower grades, fewer extracurricular activities, burnout and less interest in school, and increased drug use or other delinquent behavior. The ideal job is eight to ten hours a week, allowing time for school, activities, and sleep.

Simple Budgeting

Hurwitz, Jane. *High Performance Through Effective Budgeting.* New York: Rosen, 1996. Basic information on budgeting at home, at school, at a job, and for the future. Includes a list for further reading.

Kyte, Kathy S. *The Kids' Complete Guide to Money.* New York: Knopf, 1984. Tips on advertising awareness, budgeting, earning, consumer awareness, making do with less, and having fun without spending a fortune.

For Further Exploration

Grand, Gail l. Free (and almost free) *Adventures for Teenagers.* New York: J. Wiley, 1995. Exciting opportunities for teenagers (and sometimes younger) to expand their knowledge in humanities, science, math, technology and other fields of interest by attending free (or under $200) programs or internships offered by a variety of colleges, state agencies and other educational outlets. Many programs are targeted towards women and minorities, and most are offered during the summer months. Indexed by state and area of interest.

Malinchak, James. *From College to the Real World: How to Land Any Job You Desire Right Out of College.* Montrose, CA: Positive, 1995. This enthusiastic job-hunting guide encourages students to gain work experience while still in college through internships, gives tips from employers on what they seek in job applicants, and pushes persistence as the key to getting the job you want.

Oldman, Mark and Samer Hamadeh. *Student Access Guide to America's Top Internships.* New York: Random House, 1995. Internship opportunities are listed alphabetically in entries containing information on the internship and how to apply, followed by indexes that list internships available to high school students, those that offer scholarships or free housing, which are most competitive, those available during the summer, and other categories such as location.

Peterson's Internships 1996: Over 35,000 Opportunities to Get Experience in Today's Competitive Job Market. 16th ed. Princeton, NJ: Peterson's, 1995. Listings of internship opportunities include general description, positions available, benefits, eligibility, and contact person. Indexes by field of interest and geographic area.

For Fun-Fiction!

Help Wanted: Short Stories About Young People Working. Selected by Anita Silvey. New York: Little Brown, 1997. On-the-job stories by popular authors about a dozen culturally diverse young people.

Working Days: Short Stories About Teenagers at Work. Anne Mazer, ed. New York: Persea Books, 1997. Fifteen short stories about teens in a variety of job situations.

Resources on State & Federal Labor Regulations & Laws Pertaining to Youth

To find out what laws and/or regulations apply in your area in addition to federal labor regulations, contact your local employment office by checking in the government pages of the telephone book. Look under Employment or Labor in the federal, state, and county sections. If that doesn't work, check at the library for pamphlets, state codes (laws and regulations), or addresses of state officials. (See the State Leadership Directory below.) The local branch of the Small Business Administration (SBA) can be found in the telephone book in the federal government section. As another option, employers that hire minors should have copies of the restrictions on hours for minors. Your school counseling or guidance office may have this information as well. Several states have more restricted working hours for minors than federal restrictions allow--find out what the law is for your state. The county courthouse or city hall is another possibility for finding this information--call first to find out if they have brochures or pamphlets. States, counties, and cities often have home pages now—check at the library, use an Internet guide, or use keyword searching to find them and look for employment information. Find out if a business permit or license is required for your own business by contacting the county courthouse or city hall. Some additional resources are listed below.

Federal
Agencies

U.S. Department of Labor

Internal Revenue Service (tax filing forms available at libraries and post offices)

Equal Employment Opportunity Commission

Social Security Administration (apply for a Social Security number at the local office)

Federal Laws of Interest

Fair Labor Standards Act (FLSA), Americans with Disabilities Act (ADA), Civil Rights Act of 1964 (and 1991), *Occupational Safety and Health Act, Industrial Insurance Act, Minimum Wages and Hours Act.* Check the U.S. Code (USC) or the Code of Federal Regulations (CFR) to see these laws and regulations.

State

Check with the state department listed below or ask at the library for a legal deskbook on state employment regulations such as: ***Employment in Washington: A Guide to Employment Laws, Regulations, and Practices,*** by Michael J. Killeen (Michie Law, 1996). Check your state codes (state equivalents of the USC and CFR) if available or if necessary.

State Leadership Directory: Directory III: Administrative Officials 1997. Lexington, KY: Council of State Governments, 1997. Contains official's names, addresses, phone and fax numbers for each state for the departments list below:

Child Labor—Administration and enforcement of child labor laws

Employment Services—Job counseling, testing and placement services

Equal Employment Opportunity—Enforcement of equal employment opportunity laws

Job Training—Job training and services for the unemployed, underemployed, and economically disadvantaged

Labor—Administration and enforcement of the state's labor laws

Occupational Safety—Enforcement of safety standards for employees and employers

Glossary of Terms

application - a form requesting information for employment.

applicant - person applying for employment.

availability - when you are available to work.

clerical - office work.

commission - an amount of money, such a percentage of a product's selling price, paid for services.

commitments - obligations

employee - a person who works for another person or company.

employer - a person who hires people to work for him or her.

I-9 - a federal form used to determine an employee's citizenship.

internship - a student in supervised training on a job.

interview - a face-to-face meeting between an applicant and an employer.

mentor - an advisor who offers encouragement and assistance to a less experienced person.

minimum wage - the lowest wage that can be paid for work by law.

nonverbal - a message given without the use of words.

overtime - hours in excess of 40 per week.

recommendation - a written or oral confirmation of an individual's competence or character.

reference - a person who recommends another for employment.

reimburse - to pay back to someone.

resign - quit.

resume - a written summary of one's qualifications and work experience.

scholarship - money awarded to a student.

seasonal - work for under 90 days, usually during the summer only or holidays.

supervisor - boss.

telemarketing - selling something over the telephone.

temporary - for a limited time.

terminated - end employment.

volunteer - to work without receiving pay.

W-2 - a federal form that is provided to an employee by an employer reporting the individual's annual income, taxes, and miscellaneous deductions. The employee is required to return the form when the individual files his or her income tax form with the U.S. Internal Revenue Service (IRS).

W-4 - a federal form to be used to designate the number of income tax deductions claimed by an employee.

W-5 - a federal form required to establish eligibility for Earned Income Credit (EIC). These are benefits granted to low income parents of dependent children.

Work permit - a state form required for employment of under age students.

Index